Inclusion Is Dead

Inclusion is Dead is a provocative polemic against the widely held notion that inclusion for all children and young people with SEN is both possible and desirable. For those with severe learning difficulties (SLD) and profound and multiple learning difficulties (PMLD), the authors argue, it is neither.

Imray and Colley assert that the dominance of inclusion has meant that there has been no serious attempt to look at the educational difficulties faced by learners with PMLD and SLD. As a vision of egalitarianism and equality for all, they say, educational inclusion is dead.

The authors controversially believe that unless education changes, it will remain as a disabling institution that does the exact opposite of its intention. The book presents the argument that theorists of inclusion have failed to provide practical solutions on how inclusion can be achieved when SLD and PMLD learners are involved, as well as discussing the drawbacks of the 'inclusion for all argument'.

With up-to-date references throughout, *Inclusion is Dead* will be an insightful read for teachers and SENCO trainers, as well as postgraduates and undergraduates studying courses on politics, philosophy, and society.

Peter Imray is a freelance trainer, advisor, and writer in the area of special educational needs.

Andrew Colley is Senior Lecturer in Special Education at the University of East London, Cass School of Education and Communities.

Inclusion is Dead
Long Live Inclusion

Peter Imray and Andrew Colley

Routledge
Taylor & Francis Group

LONDON AND NEW YORK

First published 2017
by Routledge
2 Park Square, Milton Park, Abingdon, Oxon OX14 4RN

and by Routledge
711 Third Avenue, New York, NY 10017

Routledge is an imprint of the Taylor & Francis Group, an informa business

© 2017 Peter Imray and Andrew Colley

British Library Cataloguing-in-Publication Data
A catalogue record for this book is available from the British Library

Library of Congress Cataloging-in-Publication Data
A catalog record for this book has been requested

ISBN: 978-1-138-24159-6 (hbk)
ISBN: 978-1-138-28214-8 (pbk)
ISBN: 978-1-315-28005-9 (ebk)

Typeset in Times New Roman
by Apex CoVantage, LLC

Contents

1 Setting the scene

The fundamental premise of this book is that educational inclusion, despite a constantly changing and liquid definition, has not been achieved in any country under any educational system despite some 30 years of trying. It was no doubt a valiant and laudable attempt to ensure justice and equity but its failure must now be addressed. Inclusion has become a recurring trope of academic writing on education; it is trotted out as an eternal and unarguable truth, but it is neither. It doesn't work, and it never has worked. Inclusion is dead.

We contend that for two small but significant groups of learners with severe learning difficulties (SLD) and profound and multiple learning difficulties (PMLD) who combined make up around 50,000 of the school population in England alone (Pinney, 2017),[1] educational inclusion, when defined as working in the same school and/or in the same classroom and/or working on the same curriculum, not only hasn't worked, it is also positively harmful since it directly reduces the opportunity for learners to learn and wastes extraordinarily precious and expensive learning time. There are, in addition, very strong arguments for assuming that these 50,000 who make inclusion for all as a workable concept impossible are only the tip of the iceberg. It may be that education is not working for a considerably higher percentage of the United Kingdom's school population, that this can be directly laid at the door of the dominant inclusive pedagogy and that this is also likely to be the case in most Western First World economies.

One of the reasons for the systemic educational failure of learners with SLD and PMLD in inclusive educational models is because either insufficient, or more commonly, no thought has been given to pedagogical considerations, which involves asking why we might be educating those with SLD and PMLD in the first place.

The emphasis on education as the primary means of attaining a socially inclusive society by insisting pupils learn the same things in the same classroom is mistaken. Rather, education needs to be seen as a means of fostering pupils' opportunities to maximise their potential to do the very best they can do and to be the very best they can be, irrespective of their individual level of disability. In other words we strongly advocate adopting a Capabilities Approach (Sen, 1992, 1999, 2005; Nussbaum, 2004, 2006, 2011). The authors fully accept that their views are principled and political. They recognise that there is very little research into the learning of those with SLD and PMLD which might uphold their views, but that is because there is very little research into the learning of those with SLD and PMLD to uphold any views about anything. The authors have therefore (with a combined 50 years of experience in the classroom) taken their experience of practice first and worked outwards from there. Of primary interest to the authors is firstly what works and what doesn't work and secondly why it works and why it doesn't work. We accept the criticisms of Bratlinger (1997) that, as with previous questioners of inclusion as a satisfactory educational doctrine, we cannot lay claim to objectivity and neutrality; it is our opinion, just as proponents of inclusion are expressing their opinion.

We trust, however, that the extensive and detailed arguments put forward in this book will give all at least pause for thought, especially since we adopt the position that we have expertise in the field of SLD and PMLD and our opinion, as experts, carries weight. When looking at inclusive pedagogy, Davis and Florian (2004) admired the abilities of a number of teachers who were able to span a considerable breadth of expertise and knowledge and wondered if we could all learn from them:

> Expert teachers who respond to the diversity of learners' needs found in every classroom, but especially in classrooms with a high proportion of children with special educational needs, have been found to embed a responsiveness to individual need within the context of whole class teaching. What is not well understood is how they do this.
>
> (Davis and Florian, 2004, 36)

We think the clue lies in the wording – they are 'expert' teachers. Many commentators have written on the imperfect state of inclusion, yet whichever country and educational system is being discussed, a common theme is the generally unspoken but sometimes quite specific criticism of teachers for not being able to do what some, the 'expert teachers', can clearly do (for example in the United Kingdom: Hart and Drummond, 2014; Florian and Black-Hawkins, 2011; in the United States: Jackson, 2014; Ryndack et al., 2013; in Australia: Slee, 2010; Conway, 2012).

> Knowing the limits of one's knowledge and skill and being given the responsibility for refusing clients whose problems don't match one's

training and skills are rather basic professional and moral responsibilities, it seems to me. Those who do not want teachers to decline to teach a child for whom they are not prepared believe one of two erroneous things. . . . (a) teachers shouldn't be professionals in any true sense or (b) students don't actually differ much in what's required to teach them. Teaching is teaching, they seem to believe, and if you can teach one student you can teach any student. I find that kind of denial maddening.

(Kauffman, 2002, 250)

We argue that the philosophy and practice of teaching those on the SLD and PMLD spectrums is not just a matter of differentiation, it is fundamentally different. This leads to the inevitable conclusion that we ought to be teaching them differently and, indeed, teaching them different things. It is neither possible nor desirable to do this in an inclusive classroom.

One of the major reasons for the difference relates to the 'why' of education and an acceptance of education as a means to an end rather than as an end in itself. Learning may be an end, but education is a means to an end. Those with SLD and PMLD have the right to be equal members of society, to be socially included as equal citizens, to belong, to be part of rather than apart from society. When, however, the goals of education have nothing to do with what is meaningful to people, we further compound both their failure and society's failure. People with learning disabilities have the right to a voice which is their voice, not ours. We have to help them find that voice.

We do, however, have the opportunity to rectify these wrongs, even though there are no quick-fix solutions. We therefore call for the adoption of a Capabilities Approach within and beyond education which can at least set us on the right path to allow social inclusion to arise from the wreckage of educational inclusion, so that we may declare inclusion is dead: long live inclusion.

Note

1 Because both writers are British, it is natural that the essence of our arguments will come from a UK perspective. We have tried, however, to refer to the North American, Australian, and Italian experiences to act as broader examples as much as we are able and we believe that the principle arguments relating to the unworkability of inclusion as an educational concept apply equally across all First World economies.

2   What is educational inclusion?

It is widely accepted (for example, Ainscow, 2006; Garrick Duhaney, 2012; Anderson and Boyle, 2015) that the Salamanca Statement of 1994 acted as a major catalyst in the drive for inclusive education systems across the world. Inclusive institutions are, it stated,

> the most effective means of combating discriminatory attitudes, creating welcoming communities, building an inclusive society and achieving education for all; moreover, they provide an effective education to the majority of children and improve the efficiency and ultimately the cost-effectiveness of the entire education system.
>
> (UNESCO, 1994, 10)

In the United Kingdom, this more or less coincided with the election of the first Labour government for 18 years in 1997, whose education policy included a drive towards full inclusion and a decrease in separate, special school provision, though succeeding governments (including succeeding Labour governments) have drawn back from this commitment (Norwich, 2012). In the United States, numerous acts of legislation began with the *Individuals and Disabilities Act* (IDEA) of 1975, which promised the concept of 'least restrictive environment' where students with disabilities would be educated in the setting least removed from the general education classroom (Mastropieri and Scruggs, 2010). This legislation has been continually updated by, for example, the *No Child Left Behind Act* of 2001, enabling the claim that 'the history of education in the United States has demonstrated a continuing development towards greater equality and inclusivity' (Michaud and Scruggs, 2012, 23). Italy, notably, have claimed a fully inclusive education system since the 1970s and Australia have recently (from 2009 onward) moved towards a National Curriculum and national testing and assessment arrangements which have brought all schools' pupils under a common framework.

Nonetheless, despite several decades spent working towards a fully inclusive education system in all four of these countries (and we would suggest that the difficulties experienced are largely symptomatic of many other country's journeys), the inclusion project is still only 'ongoing' (Slee, 2012).

One of the major problems has been in defining exactly what inclusion is, or indeed might be, but whatever it is, there seems little doubt that it is a political and philosophical stance rather than a purely educational one (Norwich and Lewis, 2005). Norwich (2012) takes up an argument initially propounded by Cigman (2007) in seeing political differences along a continuum which covers the range of views from universal inclusion to moderate (or as Norwich terms it) 'optimal' inclusion.

> In education *[inclusion]* is the possibility of fundamental transformation of schools to respond to all differences and that categories of difference (such as special educational needs or disability) can be abandoned, as they are socially constructed and therefore not 'real'. In this analysis 'universalists' tend to hold on to the promise of possibility, while 'moderates' do not.
>
> (Norwich, 2012, 63)

It is interesting to note the language used here, where 'optimal' and 'moderate' – both good, positive words – are used to define an inclusion model that does not insist upon all children in the same class in the same school. Lauchlan and Greig (2015) carry on the premise by asking (but not answering) the question of whether inclusionists might now consider it acceptable for special schools to be part of an inclusion agenda rather than anathema to it, as Cigman's universalists still contend. Lauchlan and Greig look at the evidence from the perspective of pupils, teachers, and parents in relation to both the social and educational benefits, but come to no firm conclusion, since one study for not recognising special schools as having a role to play is generally counterbalanced by another that says the opposite. On the whole, Lauchlan and Geig's literature review confirms other findings (Topping, 2012; Norwich, 2012 for example) that the jury is still out and more research is needed. Mary Warnock, herself the great driving force towards an integrated model in the United Kingdom in the 1970s (Warnock, 1975), is now of the view that 'all children under one roof' is neither feasible nor desirable, and that we should be much more concerned with including all children in the 'common goal of education', in whatever educational setting suits them best (Warnock, 2005).

If the notion of including all children in terms of being in the same class, in the same school, being taught the same curriculum as all other children (Katz et al., 2012; Boyle and Topping, 2012) might be considered to be at one end of Cigman's (2007) spectrum of inclusion, it would seem that the notion of '*inclusive special education*' Hornby (2015) could well be at the other end. Hornby takes up Warnock's call for a much wider view of inclusion and answers many of the criticisms of Warnock by Brahm Norwich, especially in relation to issues which Norwich considered to be valid in principle but not fully thought through (Norwich, 2010). For Hornby (2015) it is clear that the universalist view is no longer relevant, noting a number of studies to support this line (for example, Evans and Lunt, 2002; Thomas and Loxley, 2007; Hansen, 2012; Kauffman and Badar, 2014a). For Hornby, such studies indicate that it is

> now widely recognised that the policy of 'full inclusion', with its vision of all children being educated in mainstream classrooms for all or most of their time at school is impossible to achieve in practice.
>
> (Hornby, 2015; 236)

Drawing heavily on the work of Kauffman and Badar (2014a, 2014b), Hornby identifies a number of 'confusions' regarding the drive for inclusive education which have seriously affected its direction and pace of travel, and have resulted in numerous wrong turns. As a result, Hornby argues, a new theory is needed to drive inclusion in a more realistic direction.

> The definition of **inclusive special education** encompasses a synthesis of the philosophies and practices of both inclusive education and special education. It involves educating children with SEND in the most inclusive settings in which their special educational needs can be met effectively, using the most effective instructional strategies, with the overarching goal of facilitating the highest level of inclusion in society post-school for all young people with SEND.
>
> (Hornby, 2015, 239, original emphasis)

Hornby's (2015, 248) pragmatic take on a typical inclusion continuum includes:

- mainstream class with differentiation of work by the class teacher;
- mainstream class with guidance for the teacher provided by a specialist teacher;
- mainstream class with support for the pupil from a teaching assistant;
- mainstream class with some time spent in a resource room;
- special class within a mainstream school;
- special class that is part of a special school but is attached to a mainstream school;

- special school which is on the same campus as a mainstream school;
- special school on a separate campus;
- residential special school on its own campus.

On the whole we welcome this approach, note that it can be fitted into America's *No Child Left Behind Act* of 2001 and the *Individuals With Disabilities Education Improvement Act* (IDEA) of 2004 with its 'least restrictive environment' philosophy, and find difficulty in arguing with any of it.

However, the above 'typical inclusion continuum' is pretty much reflective of the English special educational needs continuum as it stands today, and not even the dovest of inclusion doves would consider England to have the perfect educational inclusive system, or indeed even *an* inclusive educational system. Hornby's take on proceedings may be interesting, but it is questionable whether it constitutes inclusion.

Models of disability: the medical and social models

It is worth going back to basics with this discussion if only briefly, and the authors must at this point beg the readers' indulgence as the ground is prepared for the arguments to come. Such preparation centres on our insistence that the natures of severe learning difficulties and profound and multiple learning difficulties are academically and therefore educationally defining. That is, that the conditions of SLD and PMLD automatically limit what the child, young person, or adult can learn and how they might learn it. This has major implications for what we teach, how we teach, and, indeed, where we teach it.

For seasoned inclusionists such a statement more than probably sounds the alarm bell of yet another ringing of the medical model, or deficit model, or psycho-medical model as Hodkinson (2016) terms it, or the individual model (Oliver, 1996), or, even more emotively, the 'individual tragedy' model (Slee, 2012). What we will term throughout (for brevity's sake) as the medical model can be seen to be the position taken where special educational needs are deemed to arise from the individual's physiological, neurological, and/or psychological deficits (Skidmore, 1996). Such deficits are measured against developmental or functional norms in areas such as cognition, motor skills, speech and language, physical, behaviour, and social and emotional understanding.

Loreman et al. (2010) regard the medical model as one where

- the evidence gathered typically involves assessments (which) take place outside of the context in which the learning takes place;
- professionals suggest alternative solutions;

- the solutions may be a programme that is delivered separately from the rest of the student's peers;
- the programme is usually not consistent with curriculum models being employed within the school and therefore unlikely to transfer easily to classrooms and integrate with existing programmes.

(Loreman et al., 2010, 25)

The term 'medical model' seeks to label the learner, a philosophy rejected by many inclusionists as being a social construct which neutralises the individual and places the person in a category. The person is no longer a person, she is the category, being defined by her SEN or SLD or dyslexia, so that she then becomes the label, she then becomes disabled. The antithesis of this is the 'social model', which recognises that society's views of norms, normality, and disability place barriers to accessibility in the way of individuals who fit outside these norms (Goering, 2010).

The aim of the social model is to undermine the idea that disability is caused by bodily impairment.

(Hodkinson, 2016, 27)

Such a view differentiates impairment from disability and recognises these two things as separate, so that impairment is

lacking part or all of a limb, or having a defective limb, organ or mechanism of the body; and disability is the disadvantage or restriction of activity caused by a contemporary social organisation which takes no or little account of people who have physical impairments and thus excludes them from participation in the mainstream of social activities.

(Oliver, 1996, 22)

Since disability is culturally produced and socially structured (Oliver, 1990), individuals, whatever their impairment, must be seen as people, as individuals, with equal, inclusive, and inviolable rights if we are to value a civilised society. With inclusion comes the language of equity and fairness and morality, for the opposite is exclusion, as the opposite of integration is segregation. Acceptance of the social model, argues Ekins (2015), compels all schools to move to a more inclusive (social) model where there is:

- understanding that the difficulty is not the child, rather it is the barriers impacting on the child;
- a focus on removing barriers to learning and participation;

- an emphasis on individual approaches;
- involvement of the pupil in discussions and review of progress and provision.

(Ekins, 2015, 175)

Given that the term medical model is derogatory, invented by opponents of labelling, it is hardly surprising that it is universally held in such low esteem. It gave rise, argues Reiser (2014), to the premise that it is the disabled person who cannot learn, that she is the problem and needs to be fixed. Such fixing can only come about by excluding the individual and releasing her into the hands of professionals in segregated settings who will attempt to cure, normalise, treat. Corbett and Norwich (2005) point out the moral 'wrongness' of concentrating on what someone cannot do rather than what they can do; Courtade et al. (2012) argue that we do not yet know the potential of students with severe disabilities; and, for Lewis (1991), the employment of the medical model lets schools 'off the hook' by placing the causation of the problem with the pupil rather than the learning context, and dehumanises the learner whose central life decisions are now being made by others.

This latter issue particularly has given rise to the emergence of the disability movement perspective by which disabled people themselves have sought to take back their human rights to be fully included within society (Hodkinson, 2016) and through this to the affirmative model (Swain and French, 2004) and the rights-based model (CSIE, 2008).

On the labelling and categorisation criticisms of the medical model

Lauchlan and Boyle (2007) conducted a literature review on whether the use of labels in special education was helpful or not. As strong inclusionists, it is hardly surprising that they were sceptical about the positive elements of labelling, and echoing Gillman et al. (2000), came to the conclusion that

> Those working in special education need to adopt an ethical framework to the application of labelling, one which can be considered valuable, not in terms of whether the labels are **accurately applied,** but in terms of whether it opens [and not closes] doors and creates opportunities for the person concerned.
>
> (Lauchlan and Boyle, 2007, 41, original emphasis)

On the whole we regard this as being a reasonable demand, since all things related to education, including labelling, have to be in the learners' long-term interests. That is, the label of a learner being within either the PMLD spectrum or the SLD spectrum has to lead to the establishment of an appropriate pedagogy, teachers pursuing a curriculum, and class staff applying specific skills and expertise that will allow learners to educationally do the best that they can do and be the best that they can be. However, the problems associated with the inaccurate and vague application of labels, especially by those who intrinsically distrust and reject the whole issue of labelling, can mean that learners are pushed through the wrong doors in the first place. In 2012, Ginevra Courtade and colleagues took Kevin Ayres and colleagues to task for proposing that focusing on functional skills for students with 'severe disabilities', rather than fully including them in a general education (academic) curriculum, leads to a more independent life. Both Courtade et al.'s and Ayres et al.'s perspectives on this issue are discussed later, but we want at this stage to focus on the term 'severe disabilities', which for Courtade and colleagues refers to

> students with moderate/severe intellectual disabilities who may also have physical disabilities, sensory disabilities, or autism.
>
> (Courtade et al., 2012, 3)

Whatever the merits of the arguments, the conflation of moderate learning difficulties and severe learning difficulties can only lead to confusion and inexactitude, since although these two groups clearly meet at the edges, they have quite different academic potential, in the same way that those with SLD and PMLD have quite different academic potential. We have little doubt that most of those with moderate learning difficulties are able to access an academic curriculum and some may achieve (at least early levels of) functional literacy and numeracy (Frederickson and Cline, 2015). In this case, elements of an academic curriculum might well be relevant, and they might well experience this in a conventional mainstream classroom studying a Common Core State Standards (CCSS) model, similar to both the UK and Australian National Curriculums. Such arguments however, hold no merit for those with severe learning difficulties, at least once such a diagnosis has been firmly established, since the upper reaches of their academic abilities will only surface in the very lowest reaches of such an academic curriculum model, irrespective of their age and the brilliance of the teaching. Labelling, and even more importantly, exact labelling, therefore carries significance when attempting to ascertain the nature of a curriculum that is fit for purpose.

In other arguments against labelling, much is made of the personalisation imperative, so that, for example, a ' *favourite recollection is when a teacher said in a meeting that his pupil was more David than Down's*', meaning of course that '*the child's character, individual experiences and support network were of far more importance than the medical diagnosis*' (Briggs, 2016, 11). This does of course assume that David's learning style, his character, personality, and individual experience have not been shaped by his learning difficulty, though it is impossible to know if this is so and, if it is so, by how much.

In a similar vein, Trussler and Robinson (2016) reported on a study by Robinson (2014) which asked both student teachers and experienced practitioners to imagine that they had a child named Katy in their class with a label of Down's Syndrome. They were then asked to prioritise the following questions, that in order to teach Katy effectively, did practitioners need to have in depth knowledge of (a) Down's Syndrome (b) Katy (c) how to assess and teach all children effectively? There was general agreement that b) and c) were the most important issues and, though a knowledge of Down's Syndrome might be useful as 'background information', it was not regarded as essential.

The problem here is that Robinson was asking the wrong question, since although knowledge of Down's Syndrome can be useful (there are certain very common elements of the condition that can make verbal communication very difficult for some, for example), the actual intellectual, reasoning, and cognitive variations of the condition are quite considerable. Whilst most learners with Down's Syndrome fall within the mild to moderate range of learning difficulty (Chapman, 2003), it would be not be at all unusual for Katy to have a severe or even (much less commonly) a profound learning difficulty. So for teachers to have knowledge of c) how to assess and teach *all* children *effectively*, Katy's teachers would need to have deep and meaningful knowledge of how to teach children with mild, moderate, severe, *and* profound learning difficulties. This is not impossible, but it is a very big ask, and it would be an exceptionally experienced and well-read teacher who would have 'in-depth knowledge' of all four levels of learning difficulty. A considerably more meaningful option would therefore have related to the degree of Katy's learning difficulty rather than her Down's Syndrome.

Assuming, for the sake of argument, that Katy had severe learning difficulties, Robinson (2014) might have asked her respondents to prioritise the need to have in-depth knowledge of (a) severe learning difficulties (b) Katy (c) how to assess and teach all children effectively. In this scenario, it becomes much more difficult to dispense so easily with one of the options. And now let's add in another layer of complication and assume that Katy has been diagnosed with Down's Syndrome, severe learning difficulties, and autism. Are Robinson's practitioners going to so easily reject the necessity of in-depth knowledge of autism, because they would be very well advised to proceed with a great deal of caution if they were (Jordan, 2005).

The point about this scenario is that there seems to be an assumption from proponents of the social model that in-depth knowledge of generic conditions such as severe learning difficulties (or autism for that matter) precludes, or at least is considerably less important than, looking at the learner as an individual; that knowing about Katy as an individual will give many more answers to the teacher than knowing about severe learning difficulties. But let's take the analogy a stage further. Let us assume that Katy does not have Down's Syndrome, does not have a learning difficulty, and is studying physics. Now the options are, in order to teach Katy effectively, is it important for the teacher to know about (a) physics (b) Katy (c) how to assess and teach all children effectively?

Lorna Wing's oft-quoted observation of '*show me one child with autism and I will show you one child with autism*' is equally applicable to both severe and profound learning difficulties. That is, whilst each learner with autism is bound to be different (as all children are different from each other), a deep and meaningful understanding of autism is essential if we are to be successful teachers of children, young people, and adults with autism, as Wing would have been the first to acknowledge.[1] As it is with autism, so it is with both SLD and PMLD. Knowledge that a child has severe learning difficulties is extraordinarily useful if one knows about SLD (but not very useful if one doesn't). Even more helpful is the knowledge about roughly where the learner is within the SLD spectrums, which an in-depth and working knowledge of the P scales[2] can provide. Both the curriculum and the teaching of that curriculum may well be very different at one end of the SLD spectrum (P4) to that applied at the other end of the spectrum (P8). Equally, the way children learn and what they are likely to be able to learn will be very different from one end of the spectrum to the other. Teachers are, however, highly unlikely to have an in-depth knowledge of the P scales if they do not already have an in-depth knowledge of SLD.

It is a central tenet of this book that knowledge of SLD and PMLD is at least as complicated and necessary to effective teaching of those on the SLD and PMLD spectrums as knowledge of subject is to those teaching at higher school (in UK terms, 'A' level) and possibly even undergraduate level. Teaching children, young people, and adults with SLD and PMLD is very different from other categories of disability and very different from teaching neuro-typical, conventionally developing learners (Imray and Hinchcliffe, 2014). If the teaching is very different, teachers need to know very different things.

Opponents of labelling continue however to run into conceptual cul-de-sacs. Anderson and Boyle (2015), for example, urge that funding (in Australia) should be allocated on a needs basis, thus eliminating the current reliance on labelling and categorisation. There is, however, no explanation of what to do about the organisational nightmare that ensues, since without categorisation there can be no benchmark against which funding decisions can be made. Surely it is not feasible, whatever the political will, to have several tens of thousands of claims for additional funding without any benchmarks other than individual need. This seems to be an example of Terzi's (2010) observation that in claiming that disability is squarely socially caused, the social model theorists are surely 'over-socializing' their position.

The deep-rooted distrust of labelling and categorising can result in, if not misinformation, then certainly disinformation, so that, for example, Rose and Howley (2006) are sceptical of labels, since

> the overgeneralisation of pupil needs on the basis of a special needs label is not helpful to teachers attempting to provide effective learning opportunities.
>
> (Rose and Howley, 2006, 4)

Here, 'overgeneralisation' is defined as assuming that one child with a diagnosis of, say, ASD or ADHD is going to be same as another child with ASD or ADHD. Well of course they're not! Why would they be? Anyone who has been teaching for longer than five minutes will quickly work out that children (rather like the rest of us) are different from each other.

This aversion to labels (except in the sense that one needs to avoid them) and insistence upon the philosophical and moral merits of the social model may be why, in books entitled *Special Educational Needs in the Inclusive Primary Classroom* (Briggs, 2016), *Inclusive Practice in the Primary School* (Trussler and Robinson, 2016), and *Meeting Special Needs in Primary Classrooms* (Rose and Howley, 2007), there were only two mentions of PMLD and one of SLD in the combined indexes. Trussler and Robinson (2016) on the other hand saw fit to give 27 index references to labels and labelling in their book alone.

It seems to be the case that the social model's refusal to consider labelling arises from the tendency (certainly in the past but also today) towards stigmatisation and denigration of the individual(s) so labelled. This may be so, but the answer does not lie in pretending that differences don't exist in any generic form but only as individual differences to be celebrated (Florian, 2010a) within a truly inclusive 'personalisation agenda' (Ekins, 2015, 97), since this denies our basic instinct and common-sense approach to having 30 'different' children in front of us waiting to be taught. Teachers cannot, and we would suggest, should not, teach 30 individual lessons, but will rely on generic information and broad ability groupings; it is our natural tendency as rational beings (Kauffman, 2002; Imray and Hinchcliffe, 2014). If there are pupils in the class with SLD or PMLD, teachers *will* want to know this and indeed can only teach effectively if (i) they do know this and (ii) they have a deep and meaningful understanding of the learning difficulty which applies.

The reality is that

> children with SEND attract labels from other children and teachers even when they are not formally identified as having SEND. So being stigmatised is not necessarily a result of the identification or labelling but is related to the fact that having a special educational need/disability marks them out as different from other children in some way.
>
> (Hornby, 2015, 240)

Avoiding identifying and labelling children with SEND will not prevent them from being stigmatised, but it may prevent them from getting the education that they need (Ayres et al., 2011; Kauffman and Badar, 2014b) since it might well present limits in teachers' understanding of children's difficulties (Terzi, 2010).

> One of the key difficulties in any discussion about 'SEN' . . . is the embedded assumption that there is a need to identify 'SEN' as different from what is 'normal' or 'normally accepted'. Whether we do this in well intentioned ways or not, what is implied in such an approach is an outdated, hierarchical notion that there is a 'normal', that 'we' are part of that 'norm', and that others outside of that are therefore different.
>
> (Ekins, 2015, 94)

The problem with the above and similar statements (Runswick-Cole, 2011; Hart and Drummond, 2014; Goodley et al., 2015, for example) is the implicit pejoration of both tone and language. Pejorative in the insistence that those who regard generic difference as being inevitable might well be 'well intentioned' though they are still, of course, wrong. In the notion that recognition of difference from the norm is outdated, in much the same way as racism or sexism might be. In the concept that there might even be a norm, and the placing of such words as 'norm' and 'normal' inside inverted commas to indicate how bizarre these words really are. In the view that this idea is automatically hierarchical, as though the holders of such a view axiomatically regard those outside of the norm as being inferior to themselves. The ignorant might think this, but in the immortal words of Dilbert, 'since when did ignorance become a point of view?' (Adams, 2001).

Of course words such as norm and normal are relative and contextual. What is normal in one situation or society or setting may not be in another.

Words that are relational clearly suffer from clarity at certain points, and words such as normal are open to misuse and abuse; they must be used and treated with care. But the word normal still exists and has real meaning, unlike that other more infamous 'n' word. We must think very carefully about stopping using words simply because they have been mistreated in the past and we certainly can't base a whole pedagogy around the notion that there are certain words that are unpalatable to our modern, Western, liberal sensibilities. To repeat Terzi's (2010) warning, if we deny any reference to the norm, that is, typical human functioning, how can we evaluate impairment and disability, and thereby distribute resources accordingly?

Let us be very clear on this: learners with SLD and PMLD do not learn in normal ways; their learning is abnormal in the sense that they learn very, very differently from the vast majority of learners and this can be very worrying and perplexing for very many stakeholders, not least the person themselves. This is however neither undesirable nor distasteful nor deviant nor freakish; it is what it is. Not putting a label on it does not make it go away.

Surely the way to overcome negative and stigmatising labels is to prove that individuals who suffer from impairments can be successful in both education and society, but they will not be able to be successful in education until an appropriate pedagogy and curriculum is arrived at and specialists in SLD and PMLD are given time to develop both ideas and practice. We have no doubt that labelling is an issue in the wider society of the United Kingdom and evidence of this seems to abound in the world of work where only 5.8% of people with learning disabilities were in paid employment in 2016 (Mencap, 2016), but this is a problem (discussed more fully in Chapter 8) which the whole of society needs to urgently address.

Success in society and the quality of an individual's life is dependent on a number of supporting attitudes and agencies, but individuals with impairments are likely to be disabled if they meet with failure in education. The two are inextricably linked. Curricula development must at least, in part, be driven by how we envisage those with SLD and PMLD maximising their quality of life chances – what a person can do and what a person can be. Curricula development takes time; it cannot and will not happen overnight, but the starting point for SLD has not yet begun, having been effectively stifled in the United Kingdom at least, and probably in many other countries by the insistence upon a common (national) academic curriculum framework. Curriculum development for PMLD is, at least in the United Kingdom, slightly further along the road, but there is still a long way to go before conclusions as to its efficacy can be drawn. In the United Kingdom there are isolated pockets of good and outstanding practice in teaching children, young people, and adults with SLD or PMLD, but this has been done despite the system not because of it and there is, as yet, no cohesive understanding of where the journey might take us. Nor will there be until the journey has had a chance to get considerably further down the road.

Conclusion

Inclusion means a number of different things to a number of different people (Cigman, 2007; Terzi, 2010; Norwich, 2012; Hornby, 2015). This in itself is surely its fatal weakness, since it is very difficult, if not impossible, to see the journey towards inclusion as 'ongoing' (Slee, 2012) if there are constant disagreements about both the direction of travel and the destination. That may indeed be a reason why the journey is still ongoing, since many of the travellers have been going round in circles.

The social model is built upon the idea of liberating individuals from the imprisonment of the social construct of disability. Unfortunately, within education, the universal inclusionist interpretation of justice and equity and equality (Ainscow et al., 2012) does the exact opposite, for it interprets these words as meaning 'the same', as in the same school, the same class, and/or being taught the same curriculum. Thus those who cannot succeed in the same school, the same class, and/or being taught the same curriculum are now imprisoned within these demands. For those with SLD and PMLD, the debate must centre on ideas of pedagogy and curriculum that are fit for purpose; in succeeding chapters, we will explore more fully the notion that such learners are not best served within an academic, linear model at which they are bound, by definition, to fail. However much we attempt to adapt this model, by personalisation or differentiation or any other strategy, the model is still inappropriate and totally unfit for purpose.

Notes

1 It is the authors' contention that the increasingly common allocation of complex learning difficulties (Carpenter et al, 2015; Pinney, 2017 for example) is occasioned by duality of difficulty. Perhaps the most common of these is 'autism and.......' where a diagnosis of autism is linked to a recognition that there is likely to be an additional learning difficulty. Here the authors believe that the autism is about how one teaches, the degree of learning difficulty (or indeed the fact that there might well be no learning difficulty at all) is linked to both 'how' and 'why' pedagogical questions. It is therefore the case that where a learner has both autism and severe learning difficulties, the SLD will determine the nature of both the pedagogy and curriculum, whilst the ASD may only affect pedagogical considerations in terms of teaching strategies.'
2 The P scales are discussed in some detail in Chapter 4, '*The defining learning characteristics of PMLD and SLD*'.

3 Current perspectives and practice

In the previous chapter we discussed the complex nature of the debate around inclusive education with particular reference to the impact of the medical and social models of disability on that debate. In this chapter we will look in more detail at inclusion specifically with respect to young people with SLD and PMLD. We will draw on research and on the views of practitioners to ask if practice, attitudes, and policy have in fact included this group of learners at all or whether what Hodkinson (2012) acknowledges as 'the *clash between ideality and practicality*' (p. 7) has meant that they have been overlooked.

Brantlinger (2006, cited in Walton, 2016) notes that the ways we think about inclusive education will determine the ways we enact inclusive education, so we need to ask whether there is actually any hard evidence of the successful full inclusion of young people with SLD or PMLD in mainstream educational settings. There is a significant amount of research into inclusive practices in general, although very little which specifically focuses on SLD and PMLD. Conducting this kind of research is compromised by a number of factors, not least confusion around the meaning of inclusion, and this is likely to cloud judgements about what constitutes 'success'. In a comprehensive study of the literature around inclusive practices, Rix et al. (2009) noted that the notion of 'success' was generally judged by the researcher carrying out the study, with teachers only involved in 38% of judgements and pupils in just 19%. To muddy the waters further, the practice of inclusive education can vary significantly between and within countries, cultures, and educational systems, and this will have a further significant effect on any definition of 'successful' inclusion (Gunnþórsdóttir, 2014; Ainscow, 2005). Studying the full range of inclusive practice anywhere in the world in order to assess its effectiveness would be a monumental task and likely to be compromised further by ethical issues around access. It would also require very close scrutiny indeed of all the data, participants, beliefs, attitudes, and curricula within each environment.

Where observations have been carried out, it has been shown (Westwood, 2015) that teachers often claim to use differentiation in their classes to a much greater degree than they actually do; specifically concentrating on SLD and PMLD, Lacey and Scull (2015) have found that when observing teachers in fully inclusive settings, effective differentiation was problematic where schools do not employ sufficiently experienced and qualified specialist teachers. Lesson time can simply consist of keeping a learner with SLD or PMLD visibly busy with no real connection to the rest of the class. Lacey and Scull also observed instances of teachers not acknowledging the pupil's non-verbal vocalisations, or asking for the learner to be taken out of the room so as not to disrupt the learning of his or her peers. Understandings amongst teachers were often confusing or potentially detrimental, and in one instance it was

> difficult to get across the message that equality and inclusion is not about treating everyone the same but about identifying and mitigating individual learning barriers.
>
> (Lacey and Scull, 2015, 1)

Webster and Blatchford (2014) found that (mainstream) teachers regularly handed over responsibility for pupils with complex learning difficulties to teaching assistants (TAs), who were insufficiently qualified, trained, and experienced in the pedagogies required for the task, and as a result the pupils were more isolated from their peers and spent longer time out of class. Martin and Alborz (2014) also highlight the fact that a lack of knowledge and preparedness on the part of teaching assistants affects the extent to which students with learning disabilities can access education in both special and mainstream environments, and Webster and Blatchford found that there were significant gaps in both teachers' and TAs' knowledge for meeting the needs of these pupils:

> Most teachers reported having had no training on meeting the needs of pupils with high levels of SEN, indicating failings in initial teaching training. As TAs held valuable knowledge about the pupils they supported, teachers often positioned them as the 'expert', despite TAs having similar weaknesses in their knowledge and training.
>
> (p. 197)

The issue of appropriate training is underlined by Florian and Black-Hawkins (2011), who note that a common finding in international research literature is that teachers feel pupils with SLD and PMLD need specialist teaching which they have not been trained to provide. Carter (2015) in his review of initial teacher training (ITT) in the United Kingdom, points to a significant gap in training courses with an SEN element.

Simmons and Watson (2014) explore the school life of a 9-year-old boy with PMLD (Sam) whose week is split between a UK special school and a mainstream school for four days a week and one day a week respectively. They argue that Sam is much more 'Sam', much more alive, much more open to social interaction when he is with his peers for the one day per week in his mainstream class, which is 'success' measured in terms of social interaction. Simmons and Watson also contend that when Sam is in his special school for four days per week, he spends so much time doing switch work that he is not given any opportunity to be Sam, and his resistance to this incessant switch work is taken as evidence of his inability to master the switch task itself. The PMLD learning theory that Simmons and Watson cite to justify this conclusion, ascribed to Jean Ware (1994, 2003), seems however to be an inaccurate interpretation of her writings:

> The idea here is that if the environment consistently responds to select behaviours then people with PMLD may discover that they can influence the world around them – that is, they develop contingency awareness. It is argued that people with PMLD first need to learn that their actions have consequences in the objective world before they learn that their actions can also be meaningful to others and thus influence the social world.
>
> (Simmons and Watson, 2014, 12/13)

A quick glance at *Routes for Learning* (WAG, 2006), to which seminal document Ware was a major contributor, will affirm that contingency awareness (the understanding that a single action will lead to a particular effect) can be gained through a wide variety of cause-and-effect scenarios and it is certainly not the case that an environmental understanding precedes a social one. Rather, one might expect the route taken by the child (environmental or social) to depend upon individual motivation. What however might be happening in Sam's special school which might lead them to spend so much time on switch-based learning activities is the over-riding need to show 'success' within a linear, academic, developmental model. In other words, Sam's special school is likely to be overly reliant on a (mainstream-based) target-driven curriculum model, which typically might hit the target but miss the point, in that the target (for Sam to touch the switch) becomes the end point of education rather than the means to an end (for Sam to communicate). Interestingly the social success of Sam's one day in mainstream is freed by Simmons and Watson from being measured according to that same model. Interestingly also, this is not the first time that Ben Simmons has criticised special schools' ability to teach children with PMLD by highlighting the failings of individual children in individual special schools, but as Imray and Hinchcliffe's (2014) criticism of an earlier study by Simmons and Bayliss (2007) has pointed out, allegations of a single child failing in a special school does not constitute a theory of the educational desirability of mainstream inclusion.

Given that the predominant pedagogical model of mainstream education is linear and academic, it is hardly surprising that amongst the specific reasons (Cameron, 2014) for teachers' perceived lack of responsibility for the education of students with severe disabilities was the belief that the attention devoted to these students would disrupt the quality of instruction provided to the rest of the class. This is, in turn, inevitable, with accountability undermining inclusive education (Blower, 2015), which Gunnþórsdóttir (2014) describes as a '*tension between striving for effectiveness, on the one hand, and pressure for inclusiveness, on the other*' (p. 38). In this context, children who demand high levels of teacher support and other resources, along with students who fail to meet behavioural and cultural norms in the classroom, become unattractive clientele for schools struggling to improve standards or to evidence progress (Runswick-Cole, 2011; Robertson, 2015). Where there is participation (Lawson and Byers, 2015), it can often be no more than superficial or tokenistic, including what Hodkinson (2012) calls archly '*inclusion as spectacle*' (p. 6).

So if 'full' inclusion is difficult to achieve in practice, do practitioners actually believe in it, or are we using the notion of 'inclusion for all' without really thinking about its implications? What is clear is that beliefs are very firmly held by all sides and have led to often heated debate which has made it difficult to move practice forward (Florian, 2010b). Perhaps a more pragmatic observation is Nussbaum's (2007) contention that a theory (for example, inclusive education) may be seriously great, yet have '*serious limitations in some area or areas*' (p. 3), with Shuttleworth (2013) pointing out that practitioners and policy makers often have '*exclusion clauses*' pinned to their inclusion arguments, and can in fact quite reasonably ask who they should include and why (Allan, 2013).

Sometimes these exclusion clauses are tacit, but they almost always refer to young people with highly complex needs, such as those on the SLD and PMLD spectrums. An ideological commitment to inclusive education, for instance, has been shown to be in direct correlation to the level of resources available (Clough and Nutbrown, 2005), and if these resources are not forthcoming, it may be perfectly natural for teachers to reject the idea of the moral rightness of inclusion. With most learners with SLD or PMLD requiring very high levels of resources – not to mention additional and highly specialised training, skills, experience, use of time, and quite possibly medical support – it is no doubt these are the very pupils teachers have in mind when they struggle '*uncomfortably to articulate a growing resistance*' (Clough and Nutbrown, 2002, p. 62). Avramidis and Norwich (2002) show that a positive attitude towards inclusion can be correlated to the degree of the disability: thus teachers show willingness to include students with disabilities in line with the degree of the impairment and can be more positive towards students with mild and physical disabilities than towards those who have complex needs. There can be little doubt then (Allan, 2013) that many teachers believe that alternative, special provision suits children with complex special needs more than a placement in a mainstream setting, and this is perhaps not surprising when we consider that very often pupils with complex needs challenge even our most skilled and specialist teachers (Carpenter et al., 2015). Loreman (2013) asked teachers in training in a post-graduate educational setting heavily committed to full inclusion if there were any groups who needed to be excluded from mainstream classrooms and why they should be excluded. Whereas one-third supported inclusive classrooms, just over half justified exclusion for pupils with challenging behaviour and/or complex needs. It is these exclusion clauses in debate, research, and policy which may go some way to explaining why 'full inclusion', with its vision of all children being educated in mainstream classrooms, has not been achieved (Hornby, 2015), and initiatives to include all have largely failed to include those with SLD and PMLD (Carpenter et al., 2015).

In a detailed study, Norwich (2008) reports that education professionals in the Netherlands, United States, and England experience fundamental dilemmas occasioned by the difficulties of teaching a mainstream, neurotypical curriculum to children with special educational needs. Ware (2014) sees strong evidence that the issue in the United Kingdom of reconciling entitlement to access a common curriculum with providing for individual needs continues to provoke tensions for teachers of learners with SLD and PMLD. Her analysis of frequent discussions on the SLD Forum (http://lists. education.gov.uk/mailman/listinfo/sld-forum), an email forum for teachers of children with SLD and PMLD primarily in the United Kingdom but also used by teachers in Australia and New Zealand, suggests that the main issues for teachers are (i) doubts about the extent to which learners with SLD can be enabled to access the general mainstream curriculum, (ii) how best to support access for them, and (iii) doubts about the relevance of that curriculum to their needs. Ware's (2014) literature review relating to curriculum considerations for SLD is also interesting in the conclusion that the research which might inform best practice is often contradictory and is even more often challenging to replicate in the classroom. Her conclusion is salutary in that

> the responses of many practitioners to this group of learners reflect
> ongoing concerns that we continue to struggle (to paraphrase Wedell

(1995)) to give them access to a system which is unsuitable for them. The link between research and practice, academic debate and day to day life in the classroom often seems tenuous at best.

(Ware, 2014, 500)

Cameron (2014) studied teacher/student interactions in 'inclusive classrooms' in Ohio from Kindergarten to grade 8. These classes purported to include children with severe disabilities, but teachers reported that although children with mild disabilities attended general education classes approximately 80% of the school day, those with severe difficulties were included in mainstream classes for less than half of the school day. The teachers here also described the routine handing over of responsibility for those with SLD from teachers to 'paraprofessionals', with one class teacher describing the work of one child with SLD as '*totally separate from what we are doing*'. Cameron quite rightly asks if this phenomenon signals a movement towards a degree of 'resegregation' of students with severe disabilities and cites the US Department of Education, 2013) data showing that students with severe disabilities remain disproportionately less likely to access the general education classroom. Recent statistics from the United States suggest that only 27% of children with SLD and 18% of children with PMLD are educated in mainstream schools (Male, 2015), with the numbers falling as the pupils get older (Shogren et al., 2015), which may be related to the greater cognitive demands placed on students in secondary schools, the greater cognitive disparity as children get older, and the relative inflexibility of large schools. Gunnþórsdóttir (2014) also looks at pupils with more complex needs in her study of Icelandic teachers' discourse on inclusive education. The implementation in Iceland of an apparently highly inclusive system is meeting considerable resistance. Teachers are struggling to handle the diversity of students in their schools and, as a consequence, units or whole buildings now educate pupils within a parallel system of 'internal segregation' (Nes, 2004). Opposition to full inclusion is also reflected in Nord-Rhein Westphalen in Germany (Niemeyer, 2014), where full inclusion has become recent policy.

What though of the learners themselves? What do they think about inclusion? Pupil voice and parent voice are central to the United Kingdom's Special Educational Needs and Disability Code of Practice (2015). In fact, the very first guiding principle of the Code of Practice is that '*local authorities must ensure that children, their parents and young people are involved in discussions and decisions about their individual support and about local provision*' (p. 20, original emphasis). This is of course unarguable and, in Chapters 5, 7, and 8, we will be exploring issues around voice and agency for young people with complex needs. However, throughout the long history and praxis of inclusive education (Hodkinson, 2012), has anyone actually tried to find out what learners with SLD/PMLD think about inclusion?

There are of course, major challenges for those trying to interpret the feelings and experiences of those on the SLD and PMLD spectrums (Fergusson et al., 2015), and as a consequence they are frequently omitted from participatory research (Hill et al, 2016). Professionals may not have the resources or experience to conduct meaningful interviews (Whitehurst, 2007), and the young people themselves are likely to express themselves in ways which do not fit neatly into any recognised methods of gathering information or analysing qualitative data (Nind et al., 2010). Studies which purport to be able to reveal the attitudes of learners with SLD or PMLD towards inclusion tend to be compromised by inconsistency, or the fact that they don't actually access the opinions of young people with SLD/PMLD at all.

Shogren et al. (2015) for instance undertook a study on the perspectives of students with disabilities about inclusive schools. Focus groups were conducted with 86 students from six schools that were recognised as exemplars of inclusive school-wide practices. According to the study, each school supported students with a range of disabilities, including 'severe disabilities', to participate in general education classrooms. However, the 'Interview Guide' (p. 247) suggests that the researchers should ask questions such as '*How does your teacher help you learn*', and '*Do you ever interact with the Principal*'. The complexity of these questions suggest that the respondents could not have been classified as having PMLD according to any of the current definitions, and most with SLD would probably struggle. Researchers even admitted that the inclusion of students with more significant communication-related support needs in the study was a challenge, and those who needed extensive communication supports were not adequately represented in the sample.

Whitehurst (2007) conducted an arts project which aimed to gather the perspectives of children with profound and multiple learning difficulties on inclusion. However, as with Shogren et al., the children selected for the project did not appear to fit any recognised definitions of PMLD and certainly not the one outlined in Chapter 4. They had been '*selected to participate in the inclusion project on the basis of their ability to function well in new and challenging environments*' (p 57), and one of the young people had '*moderate verbal skills and was always chatty*' (p 59)!

In a similar vein, a dissection of the Italian experience of 'full inclusion' by Lauchlan and Fadda (2012) noted that Reversi et al. (2007) had conducted an extensive study of 173 primary and secondary schools involving 85 mainstream teachers and 88 specialist teachers, that is, those working in mainstream to support the children with disabilities. There were

36 participating schools located in three different regions of Italy and all agreed that academic and social inclusion works for everyone and was entirely positive.

> The children involved in the same study (102 disabled and 102 non-disabled) were asked to complete a questionnaire, which provided an evaluation of their social inclusion and level of loneliness at the schools . . . both disabled and non-disabled rated themselves as having a low sense of loneliness, indicating they felt socially included.
>
> (Lauchlan and Fadda, 2012, 33)

It is however, quite remarkable that children with severe learning difficulties and profound and multiple learning difficulties were actually able to complete the questionnaire. How were they able to read it and how were they able to write it? Or perhaps they had help? If so, this was unstated by Lauchlan and Fadda, but if they did have help, how did the helper define 'loneliness' and 'sense of' – both entirely abstract concepts that will be difficult even for a high-functioning learner with SLD, never mind someone with PMLD? We would in fact go so far as to say that if they could make such an independent judgement, they would not, by definition, have SLD or PMLD. It would certainly be fair to ask in the case of any of the research studies cited above if the perspective of anyone with PMLD was recorded at all.

So, it seems that the essential components of 'full' inclusion have remained elusive (Sharma and Sokal, 2015) and, with respect to the inclusion of young people with SLD and PMLD, much of the debate over the last 50 years has at best lacked clarity and purpose and at worst completely ignored these groups. This is what Nussbaum (2007) calls a '*serious unsolved problem of justice*' (p. 3) in that we still apparently have faith in inclusion for 'all', whilst at the same time collectively sidestepping the issue of children with SLD and PMLD. We don't seem to be able to admit that for tens of thousands of young learners, inclusion either hasn't worked or has not even been applied.

This hasn't meant of course that the needs of children with SLD/PMLD have not been met. Largely overlooked or misrepresented in the inclusion debate, in the United Kingdom, most have settled almost by default into special schools with English special schools for example, educating 79% of children with SLD and 81% of children with PMLD (Pinney, 2017, 38). Pinney also notes that there has been a marked and steady decline in the number of children with complex needs educated in English secondary mainstream schools, down some 22% since 2007 (p. 39). This is of course hardly surprising when we consider that effective teaching for this group is at the very least characterised by high adult-to-child ratios and individual-ised programming (Westwood, 2015), as well as a commitment to meet their basic needs for self-care, daily living, and communication, with Attwood (2013) showing that almost all children who require breathing and feeding apparatus routinely attend local special schools. In the vast majority of UK special schools, there is no doubt that young people with SLD and PMLD are well educated, well provided for, loved, respected, and supported. After all, 92% of England's special schools were rated as either good or outstanding in 2015 (38% outstanding) with only 8% requiring improvement (Ofsted, 2015). But does that mean we can rest on our laurels? Is the good educa-tion we as practitioners provide for our pupils with SLD and PMLD also the appropriate education? Simmons' and Watson's (2014) observations of 'Sam' discussed above might actually point towards the real reason why there may be a conceptual mismatch between the ideal of full inclusion and the education of pupils with SLD or PMLD: it might just lie in the nature of the linear mainstream model they are being 'invited' to be a part of whatever the setting and irrespective of the amount of apparent differentia-tion and support given.

So, what about the future? Are we going to carry on with these smoke-screens and ambiguities or will we move towards a more appropriate and realistic approach? Are the practitioners of tomorrow understanding inclu-sion in new and innovative ways? In 2016, the second author carried out a survey of the attitudes and beliefs of undergraduate students on a UK degree course in special education towards the inclusion of people with SLD and PMLD. Initially, a group of them was asked to write down an answer to the simple question: *What is inclusion?* A thematic analysis of their responses highlights the broad range of attitudes and perspectives amongst the group, with inclusion being considered to be an educational issue by only a quarter of respondents (see Figure 3.1).

Along similar lines, the students were asked to tick one statement which best summed up their understanding of inclusion (Figure 3.2), using the three following definitions:

- 'Full inclusion' to mean that all young people – regardless of their special needs – are educated in mainstream classrooms alongside their 'neuro-typical' peers (Blue).
- 'Partial inclusion' to mean that all young people – regardless of their special needs – are educated in mainstream classrooms alongside their 'neuro-typical' peers except where their learning difficulty is such that it is impractical to do so (Orange).
- 'Inclusion as a wider social issue' to mean that all young people are included in all areas of society irrespective of the school they attend (Grey).

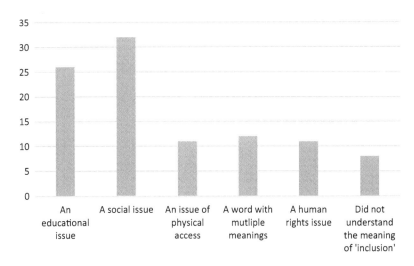

Figure 3.1 What is inclusion? (*n* = 41)

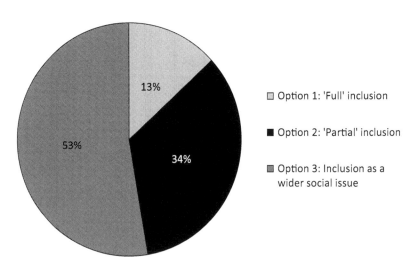

Figure 3.2 Understandings of 'inclusion': all respondents ('n' = 68)

The concept of inclusion as a wider social issue is prevalent amongst the cohort surveyed, with 'full' inclusion only supported by 13% of the respondents. A more detailed analysis of responses showed that the more the students engage with the issue, the more they feel that including learners with SLD and PMLD in mainstream settings is not feasible within current curriculum models. 'Full' inclusion is largely rejected by respondents who have had significant professional or familial experience with people with special needs, or who themselves have a learning difficulty. This rejection of notions of inclusion is even more strongly marked in those whose past experience has been with learners with SLD and PMLD or who have close familial contact with someone with SLD and PMLD. At the heart of this rejection is perhaps the feeling that schools are just not equipped and teachers not adequately trained to enact full inclusion, or as one respondent put it:

> I believe all pupils should be given the chance to be in mainstream although I believe it is not always possible through building design etc. and all staff need much better training. We need a complete overhaul of the education system and a greater focus on teacher training and attitudes being challenged.

When the students were invited to give their own definitions of inclusion (Table 3.1), we see clearly their understanding moving away from education as we know it and towards a more social model, with society leading education rather than schools acting as a model for society.

One student reminds us of a key issue: in the long history of inclusive education, we have consistently failed to acknowledge the wishes and needs of the learners themselves: '*Who said that all children with disabilities want to go to a mainstream school? It's kind of ignorant to assume this.*'

If future policy is to include learners with SLD and PMLD, we will clearly need to reflect on the attitudes of these future practitioners and look for a new paradigm to challenge familiar models and ways of thinking. Certainly a more flexible education system, or at the very least a significant

Table 3.1 Undergraduate definitions of inclusion

Inclusion is being accepted
Inclusion is being socially included within society
Inclusion is coming together
Inclusion is about social belonging and change of attitude
Inclusion is society adapting to meet the needs of the individual
Inclusion is not about the geographical location
The right to be included, have a full education, and be respected within all areas of life
All abilities having full access to all facilities in the community regardless of need
Inclusion is belonging
Including all people – races and abilities in society
Inclusion is being valued, accepted, and respected in society regardless of where you were educated
Making all individuals a part of society

restructuring of the school system, where the place of education should be less important than its content and quality (Lacey and Scull, 2015). Perhaps though what we actually need is a wider and more holistic approach where outcomes for people with SLD and PMLD will be dependent on the equal opportunities provided by the rest of society, with a philosophical shift in thinking needed to redefine what constitutes a successful and inclusive democracy.

The positioning of our most complex learners in society must be one of the key drivers for that change in approach. Anglo-Western narratives (Grove, 2012) have tended to be linear and goal directed; personhood is currently determined by agency, choice, and the capacity to contribute to economic growth under what Nussbaum (2007) calls the '*baneful influence of competition*' (p. 39). Policy across all sectors has reflected this and has certainly dominated the ways in which disability has been historically conceptualised (Goodey, 2011), with the result that those who appear to lack the capacity for self-determination, and certainly those with SLD and PMLD, have been overlooked. If we are truly to build a diverse and inclusive society, and as part of that an education system which is effective for all, we must be prepared to challenge the concept that equity equals the same, protect pluralism (Nussbaum, 2007), and '*hold complexity in our hands*' (Kearey, 2016) with a far greater acceptance of difference. Perhaps we can take a first step towards this by examining how educationally complex those with SLD and PMLD are and, indeed, exactly what these terms actually mean.

4 The defining learning characteristics of PMLD and SLD

In writing about the defining learning characteristics of those with SLD and PMLD, the authors have adopted the position that a truth is still a truth, even if it is politically unacceptable. This chapter (along with Chapters 5 and 6) therefore represent a critique of the view that all learners learn along a continuum, and can therefore be taught using the same pedagogy and the same curriculum as everybody else. For the authors, it is a truth that those with SLD and PMLD cannot, by definition, do and be certain things. In order to know what a person can do and what a person can be, it is essential to separate disability from impairment, especially when the impairment is fixed and not open to significant change. At the time of writing, it is possible to replace lost limbs, but it is not possible to replace severe or profound intellectual impairments. A detailed examination of the terms PMLD and SLD reveals their true educational meaning and examines what children within these spectrums cannot do by definition. If we know what they cannot do, we can put unachievable ideologies aside and concentrate on education supporting them towards achieving what they can do and can be. Key to this is the acceptance that:

- the learning characteristics are defining;
- though the edges may be blurred, they are not surmountable;
- the learning characteristics of these two groups are fixed within set academic parameters;
- these set parameters form essential and necessary academic frameworks for curriculum considerations.

Examples are given through a detailed look at the concepts of numeracy and literacy. There is a direct relationship between the meanings of both numeracy and literacy and why and how they are taught to neuro-typical, conventionally developing children that cannot and do not apply to either PMLD or SLD.

Learners on the PMLD and SLD spectrums form distinct and homogenous educational groupings

> The focus on deficits does not in itself define an exclusively medical model perspective and set of assumptions, especially as the deficits talked about in education are functional ones related to performances. These are different from the deficits identified in the medical diagnostic process which searches for underlying biological and other causes of these functional deficits.
>
> (Corbett and Norwich, 2005, 18)

One of the central tenets of this book is that pupils and students with severe learning difficulties (SLD) and profound and multiple learning difficulties (PMLD) form two distinct and educationally homogenous groups within the wider 'umbrella' term of Special Educational Needs. In many ways this follows on from the views put forward by Imray and Hinchcliffe (2012, 2014), who posited that a universal definition of both terms is to be found within the P scales (DfE, 2014a), which have been used extensively throughout the United Kingdom since the late 1990s, are now second nature to any UK teacher or teaching assistant working within the SLD and PMLD spheres, and deserve to be better known internationally.

The P (performance) scales were first introduced in the late 1990s by a core development team consisting of a number of leading UK academics and practitioners in the field of SLD and PMLD. Basing their writings on established research into severe and profound learning difficulties (Uzgiris and Hunt, 1975; Dunst, 1980; Aitken and Buultjens 1992; Brown, 1996; Coupe O'Kane and Goldbart, 1998, for example), the group sought to bridge the intellectual and developmental gap between birth and the start of the UK National Curriculum, which for neuro-typical, conventionally developing learners would begin at age 5 or 6.

There is little doubt that the P scales have been of enormous significance and value as an approximate and broad guide to the intellectual developmental levels that learners with PMLD and SLD are working at. Further, longitudinal research has indicated that learners with PMLD will consistently and over time stay within P1 to P3ish, whilst learners with SLD will consistently and over time stay with in levels P4 to P8ish (Ndaji and Tymms, 2009; DfE, 2011; Imray, 2013a). The 'ish' here relates to the difficulties with such definitions at the edges and it may be that a few learners on the PMLD spectrum will move into some areas of P4. Similarly, some learners on the SLD spectrum will attain in the lower, introductory reaches of the UK National Curriculum, especially when such learners have an additional diagnosis of autism, since it is common for such learners to have considerable rote learning skills which may mask, to some extent, the degree of cognitive difficulty (Jordan, 2001; Imray and Hinchcliffe, 2014; Carpenter et al., 2016).

Nonetheless, as long as those using the P scales as a guide are conscious that there will always be exceptions to the rule of PMLD being defined as P1 to P3ish and SLD being defined as P4 to P8ish, the rule still applies.

PMLD

The existing UK Department for Education definition of profound and multiple learning difficulties (PMLD) is:

> Pupils with profound and multiple learning difficulties have complex learning needs. In addition to very severe learning difficulties, pupils have other significant difficulties such as physical disabilities, sensory impairment or a severe medical condition. Pupils require a high level of adult support, both for their learning needs and also for their personal care. They are likely to need sensory stimulation and a curriculum broken down into very small steps. Some pupils communicate by gesture, eye pointing or symbols, others by very simple language. Their attainments are likely to remain in the early P-scale range (P1-P4) throughout their school careers (that is below level 1 of the National Curriculum).
>
> (DfE, 2012)

Although this definition is vague and imprecise, the key element is held in the acknowledgement that those with PMLD will be working within P1 to P4 *'throughout their school career'*, that is, up the age of 19. There is no suggestion that the term will not be appropriate for the whole of their lives.

Routes for Learning (WAG, 2006) – an assessment tool written by a number of Welsh practitioners under the guidance of Jean Ware and Verity Donnelly and a seminal work of considerable, yet concise academic rigour – notes seven key developmental milestones for those with PMLD irrespective of their age, namely:

1   Notices stimuli;
2   Responds consistently to one stimulus;
3   Contingency responding;
4   Contingency awareness;
5   Object permanence;
6   Selects from two or more items;
7   Initiates actions to achieve desired result (exerting autonomy in variety of contexts).

It might be noted that these developmental milestones occur within neuro-typical, conventionally developing babies, more or less between the ages 0 and 18 months, and might be considered to equate to Piaget's (1952) 'sensorimotor stage', his first stage of child development. The majority of those designated as having a profound learning difficulty will probably not achieve the heights described in number 7 above, and will be working at cognitive levels below this (and usually well below this) for all of their lives, but clearly this is by no means an exact science. Also, the phenomena of fractured learning and spiky profiles are well established (Carpenter et al., 2015) and some learners may be working at a number of different levels at the same time.

Whilst the UK P scales are not and cannot be related to the *Routes* milestones, we can assume that learners who are working consistently and over time at P1(i) below will probably be working at 'noticing (any) stimuli' amongst other things, whilst learners who are initiating actions to achieve desired results will be at a level of around P3 or P4.

The P levels up to P3 are generic (that is, they are not differentiated to take account of subject matter) and we have taken the liberty of reproducing them here so that those unfamiliar with them can form an opinion of the broad developmental stages covered by the term PMLD. The original (1998) P Scales document noted three broad levels (that is P1, P2, and P3), but they have since been further sub-divided to now encompass six levels.

P1 (i) Pupils encounter activities and experiences. They may be passive or resistant. They may show simple reflex responses [for example, startling at sudden noises or movements]. Any participation is fully prompted.

P1 (ii) Pupils show emerging awareness of activities and experiences. They may have periods when they appear alert and ready to focus their attention on certain people, events, objects or parts of objects [for example, attending briefly to interactions with a familiar person]. They may give intermittent reactions [for example, sometimes becoming excited in the midst of social activity].

P2 (i) Pupils begin to respond consistently to familiar people, events and objects. They react to new activities and experiences [for example, withholding their attention]. They begin to show interest in people, events and objects [for example, smiling at familiar people]. They accept and engage in coactive exploration [for example, focusing their attention on sensory aspects of stories or rhymes when prompted].

P2 (ii) Pupils begin to be proactive in their interactions. They communicate consistent preferences and affective responses [for example, reaching out to a favourite person]. They recognise familiar people, events and objects [for example, vocalising or gesturing in a particular way in response to a favourite visitor]. They perform actions, often by trial and improvement, and they remember learned responses over short periods of time [for example, showing pleasure each time a particular puppet character appears in a poem dramatised with sensory cues]. They cooperate with shared exploration and supported participation [for example, taking turns in interactions with a familiar person, imitating actions and facial expressions].

P3 (i) Pupils begin to communicate intentionally. They seek attention through eye contact, gesture or action. They request events or activities [for example, pointing to key objects or people]. They participate in shared activities with less support. They sustain concentration for short periods. They explore materials in increasingly complex ways [for example, reaching out and feeling for objects as tactile cues to events]. They observe the results of their own actions with interest [for example, listening to their own vocalisations]. They remember learned responses over more extended periods [for example, following the sequence of a familiar daily routine and responding appropriately].

P3 (ii) Pupils use emerging conventional communication. They greet known people and may initiate interactions and activities [for example, prompting another person to join in with an interactive sequence]. They can remember learned responses over increasing periods of time and may anticipate known events [for example, pre-empting sounds or actions in familiar poems]. They may respond to options and choices with actions or gestures [for example, by nodding or shaking their heads]. They actively explore objects and events for more extended periods [for example, turning the pages in a book shared with another person]. They apply potential solutions systematically to problems [for example, bringing an object to an adult in order to request a new activity].

(QCA, 2009, 8)

We wish at this stage to introduce the concept of a PMLD spectrum, with learners operating around P1 very firmly entrenched in the spectrum and those on P3 (ii) reaching the edges of it. This is not of particular consequence, other than for educators to note that those working on the edge of the spectrum may well benefit from some parts of a curriculum model applicable to those on the SLD spectrum, as well as that specifically written for those with PMLD. What is perhaps of more interest is the striking nature of the P4 hurdle, and how common it is for those on the PMLD spectrum to have extreme difficulties in scaling this hurdle. That is, there are real and marked barriers to learning (the differences between P3 and P4) which occasion *defining* learning characteristics and therefore enable the term PMLD to have real educational meaning. We are going to define these barriers as

- the ability to imitate;
- the ability to follow instruction;
- the ability to initiate proto-declarative communications;
- the achievement of a sophisticated understanding of cause and effect (contingency awareness).

Those on the PMLD spectrum will probably not have all of these abilities and may not have any; those on the SLD spectrum probably will have all of these abilities.[1] Further, this is not a matter of teaching and learning, in the sense that all of them may be learned when they are taught by skilled and experienced practitioners in exciting and motivating ways. An extremely small few of those on the PMLD spectrum may get a long way on the journey to becoming adept in all seven of the *Routes for Learning* key milestones, most will go some way, and a very small few will never get beyond the first milestone of 'noticing (any) stimuli'. We are positing however, that *all* of the barriers noted above cannot be learned by those on the PMLD spectrum and therefore cannot be taught; learners either have them, or they don't. If learners can do *all* of these things, they don't by definition, have PMLD.

SLD

The existing UK Department for Education definition of severe learning difficulties (SLD) is:

> Pupils with SLDs have significant intellectual or cognitive impairments. This has a major effect on their ability to participate in the school curriculum without support. They may also have difficulties in mobility and coordination, communication and perception and the acquisition of self-help skills. Pupils with SLDs will need support in all areas of the curriculum. They may also require teaching of self-help, independence and social skills. Some pupils may use sign and symbols but most will be able to hold simple conversations. Their attainments may be within the upper P scale range (P4-P8) for much of their school careers (that is below level 1 of the National Curriculum).

(DfE, 2012)

There are a few more problems to this definition than the one for PMLD, particularly in the use of the word 'may' rather than 'will' when considering the difficulties experienced and the requirement to teach communication, self-help, and independence. Nonetheless, as with the PMLD definition above, the key element is in the observation that their '*attainments may be within the upper P scale range (P4-P8) for much of their school careers (that is below level 1 of the National Curriculum)*'. This is still below that which a neuro-typical, conventionally developing learner would be expected to reach by the age of 5 or 6; that is, Level 1 of the UK National Curriculum. It is not unreasonable therefore to assert that those on the SLD spectrum will have cognitive abilities broadly equivalent to a range normally experience by neuro-typical, conventionally developing learners between the ages of 18 months and 5 or 6 years.

The P scales for learners working at levels at P4 and above have also been related to the various National Curriculum subjects, some of which (maths and English, for example) are further broken down into specific sub-compartmentalised areas of learning. Rather than delineate all of the P scales for all of the subjects, we have reproduced P4 to P8 in both reading and number, which will then help us to gain a broad picture of the learners' potential in the key academic areas of literacy and numeracy.

P scales 4 to 8: reading

P4 Pupils listen and respond to familiar rhymes and stories. They show some understanding of how books work, **for example, turning pages and holding the book the right way up.**

P5 Pupils select a few words, symbols or pictures with which they are particularly familiar and derive some meaning from text, symbols or pictures presented in a way familiar to them. They match objects to pictures and symbols, **for example, choosing between two symbols to select a drink or seeing a photograph of a child and eye-pointing at the child**. They show curiosity about content at a simple level, **for example, they may answer basic two key-word questions about a story.**

P6 Pupils select and recognise or read a small number of words or symbols linked to a familiar vocabulary, **for example, name, people, objects or actions.** They match letters and short words.

P7 Pupils show an interest in the activity of reading. They predict elements of a narrative, **for example, when the adult stops reading, pupils fill in the missing word.** They distinguish between print or symbols and pictures in texts. They understand the conventions of

reading, for example, following text left to right, top to bottom and page following page. They know that their name is made up of letters.
P8 Pupils understand that words, symbols and pictures convey meaning. They recognise or read a growing repertoire of familiar words or symbols, including their own names. They recognise at least half the letters of the alphabet by shape, name or sound. They associate sounds with patterns in rhymes, with syllables, and with words or symbols.

(QCA, 2009, 11; original emphasis)

P scales 4 to 8: number

P4 Pupils show an awareness of number activities and counting, **for example copying some actions during number rhymes, songs and number games; following a sequence of pictures or numbers as indicated by a known person during number rhymes and songs.**

P5 Pupils respond to and join in with familiar number rhymes, stories, songs and games, **for example, using a series of actions during the singing of a familiar song; joining in by saying, signing or indicating at least one of the numbers in a familiar number rhyme.** Pupils can indicate one or two, **for example by using eye pointing, blinks, gestures or any other means to indicate one or two, as required.** They demonstrate that they are aware of contrasting quantities, **for example 'one' and 'lots' by making groups of one or lots of food items on plates.**

P6 Pupils demonstrate an understanding of one-to-one correspondence in a range of contexts, **for example: matching objects such as cups to saucers, straws to drink cartons.** Pupils join in rote counting up to five, **for example, saying or signing number names to 5 in counting activities.** They count reliably to three, make sets of up to three objects and use numbers to three in familiar activities and games, **for example, touching one, two, three items as an adult counts, counting toys or pictures, counting out sets of three, e.g. knife, fork and spoon.** They demonstrate an understanding of the concept of 'more', **for example, indicating that more cups, counters, food items are required.** They join in with new number rhymes, songs, stories and games.

P7 Pupils join in rote counting to 10, for example, saying or signing number names to 10 in counting activities. They can count at least 5 objects reliably, **for example, candles on a cake, bricks in a tower.** They recognise numerals from 1 to 5 and understand that each represents a constant number or amount, **for example, putting correct number of objects (1 to 5) into containers marked with the numeral; collecting the correct number of items up to five.**

Pupils demonstrate an understanding of 'less', **for example, indicating which bottle has less water in it.** In practical situations they respond to 'add one' to a number of objects, **for example, responding to requests such as add one pencil to the pencils in the pot, add one sweet to the dish.**

P8 Pupils join in with rote counting to beyond 10, **for example, they say or sign number names in counting activities.** They continue to rote count onwards from a given small number, **for example, continuing the rote count onwards in a game using dice and moving counters up to 10; continuing to say, sign or indicate the count aloud when adult begins counting the first two numbers.** Pupils recognise differences in quantity, **for example, in comparing given sets of objects and saying which has more or less, which is the bigger group or smaller group.** They recognise numerals from one to nine and relate them to sets of objects, **for example, labelling sets of objects with correct numerals.** In practical situations they respond to 'add one' to or 'take one away' from a number of objects, **for example, adding one more to three objects in a box and say, sign or indicate how many are now in the box; at a cake sale saying, signing or indicating how many cakes are left when one is sold.** They use ordinal numbers (first, second, third) when describing the position of objects, people or events, **for example, indicating who is first in a queue or line; who is first, second and third in a race or competition.** Pupils estimate a small number (up to 10) and check by counting, **for example, suggesting numbers that can be checked by counting, guessing then counting the number of: pupils in a group; adults in the room; cups needed at break time.**

(QCA, 2009, 21/22; original emphasis)

There is no suggestion that the term SLD will not be appropriate for the whole of their lives and this point carries considerable significance. That is, there will probably be a number of school children, especially in the early stages of schooling, who may well be working below the starting levels of the National Curriculum but who do not have SLD. This is because, for numerous and varied reasons, such as experiencing English as a second language, or having various impairments, particularly, for example, a visual or hearing impairment which can often go undiagnosed in early childhood (Pagliano, 2001), their working within the P scales will be temporary; but they will catch up. Those on the SLD spectrum will not catch up. The definition therefore requires the additional coda of consistently, and over time, working below the academic starting point of neuro-typical, conventionally developing children.

Children and young people on the PMLD and SLD spectrums learn very differently from neuro-typical, conventionally developing learners

> We do not apologise for arguing vociferously that those with SLD and PMLD both deserve and need distinct and separate pedagogies, which in turn drives and informs distinct and separate curricula. We must get used to the idea that those with SLD and PMLD learn in fundamentally different ways from (neuro-typical) children and we must therefore teach them in fundamentally different ways.
>
> (Imray and Hinchcliffe, 2014, 24)

In confirming this position, we will concentrate our thinking on the SLD spectrum, on the basis that if we can convince the reader of the logic of the case for this group, the evidence must be irrefutable for those on the PMLD spectrum.

The defining characteristics of SLD

In recognising the defining characteristics of severe learning difficulties we acknowledge the previous work of both Lacey (2009) and Imray and Hinchcliffe (2014). These defining characteristics are:

- Consistently and over time, working academically between P4 and the starting levels of the UK National Curriculum and other similar curriculum models such as the Australian National Curriculums or a US Standards-Based Curriculum;
- Communication difficulties;
- Difficulties with abstract concepts;
- Difficulties in concentration and attention;
- Difficulties with both short-term and long-term memory;
- Difficulties with sequential memory;
- Difficulties with working memory;
- Inefficient and slow information processing speed;
- Insecure general knowledge;
- Poorly developed strategies for thinking and learning;
- Difficulties with generalisation and problem-solving.

These are not isolated difficulties but work together and upon each other to make learning extremely (or severely) problematic. Further, they are not open to being worked on in isolation but present holistically so that the solution in turn lies in adopting an holistic (rather than compartmentalised) approach to learning. It may be, for example, that educationalists might consider the difficulties with working memory as soluble and there have been a number of studies which seem to affirm this (Cowan and Alloway, 2008; Alloway et al., 2009; Klingberg, 2009; Alloway and Alloway, 2015, for example). However, such strategies that have been researched will be enormously problematic for those on the SLD spectrum since they all rely on a solid base of either language (spoken or written) and/or an understanding of abstracts in, for example, recalling a series of unrelated and de-contextualised pictures in ever more complex patterns. They further all note the inter-relationship between difficulties with working memory; short-term, long-term, and sequential memory; poor concentration and attention; and poorly developed problem-solving skills. It is noticeable that Alloway and Alloway (2015) go into some considerable detail with case studies on specific strategies that might be suitable for specific learning difficulties. Neither SLD nor PMLD feature.

Davies (2015) argues that working memory is extremely fragile, has a limited capacity, can lead to memory failure if pressed too hard, and is heavily reliant on the ability to maintain concentration and attention to the task on hand. Such overload and/or distraction leads to information being irretrievably lost from the working memory (Gathercole and Alloway, 2008), yet a sound working memory seems to be necessary for the control of attention so that the two capacities can be seen to be inseparable (Klingberg, 2009). Swanson and Jerman (2006) note that the majority of studies suggest a correlation between memory deficits and difficulties in both maths and reading, since performance depends on speedy and efficient retrieval from the long-term memory and good temporary storage is crucial when working out mathematical problems and word decoding. Further, they argue that poor recall of facts from memory increases the cognitive demands of a task, as it then has to be calculated, which in turn puts additional pressure on problem-solving strategies.

> Working memory and learning are inseparable. The importance of working memory in learning cannot be underestimated as it is a core cognitive process and predicts academic learning. Learning involves acquiring new knowledge and skills, however it is vital to remember and retain what we have learned if we are to be able to use it again and memory is the process by which we achieve this. Learning is a step-by-step process, based on the success of successive learning tasks.
>
> (Davies, 2015, 3)

Learning to be numerate

At the very earliest stages of development, Staves (2001) divides mathematical concepts into personal and social, with 'personal' being defined as having an understanding to two (as in two hands, two arms, two legs, two people bonding, etc.). 'Social' maths comes with the development of both cognitive and communication skills which allow the learner to describe quantities, space, time, and change and which will require an understanding of numbers above two. Porter (2005a) has suggested that awareness of (low) number is a basic animal trait found in many species.

Mathematics is, however, often represented within a framework of linear progression so that specific skills are learned in a set order. Maths becomes a compartmentalised subject that is further compartmentalised into number, statistics (using and applying), geometry (shape, space, and measure), data handling, algebra, etc., but because maths skills are based on establishing 'building blocks', we can't move on until the first block is learned. In numeracy for example the skill of counting is acquired first and then, in a series of building blocks placed on top of the previously learned building block, comes addition, subtraction, multiplication, division, fractions, etc. The blocks do not strictly speaking need to be taught in that order, but they are all reliant on the solid foundation of the first block: counting. A quick reference to the P scales in number, however, will inevitably lead us to the conclusion that security in number is bound to be fragile for even the highest functioning on the SLD spectrum. As a reminder, at P8, pupils will

> join in with rote counting to beyond 10, for example, they say or sign number names in counting activities. They continue to rote count onwards from a given small number, for example, continuing the rote count onwards in a game using dice and moving counters up to 10; continuing to say, sign or indicate the count aloud when adult begins counting the first two numbers.
>
> (QCA, 2009, 22)

Note the continued emphasis on laddering and scaffolding and particularly on rote counting, which of course does not imply understanding.

> Sometimes, when assessing children's calculation skills, rote learning can mask underlying procedural or conceptual difficulties. A child may **know** that '3+2 is 5', in the same way as they **know** their sister's name is Phoebe. However, it should not be assumed that the child understands **how** to add up, or what is **meant** by the word 'add'. Assessment should therefore consider children's understanding of procedures and principles as well as the ability to recall number facts.
>
> (Gillum, 2014, 279/280, original emphasis)

Gelman's and Gallistel's (1978) seminal work on the principles of understanding number has established that in order to be considered secure in number, learners must know and follow:

- the one-one principle – that one, and only one, unique number tag must be assigned to each item counted;
- the stable order principle – that count words must be produced in the same order for each count;
- the cardinality principle – that the final word of a count denotes the total number of items counted, which with typically developing children emerges at around 4 years of age (Nye et al., 2001);
- the abstraction principle – that counting can be used on any set of tangible or intangible objects;
- the order irrelevance principle – that the order in which a set of objects is counted is irrelevant.

Being numerate therefore involves recalling number names, allocating those names to each member of a group, remembering which items in a set have already been given a number, understanding the nature of a 'group', understanding that the allocated number to the last object in the group is the number given to the whole group, recognising numerals, and doing all of these things concurrently and without error. Given the enormous strain on the working memory, it is hardly surprising that the only known study relating to learners on the SLD spectrum and numeracy estimated that 80% were insecure in number (Porter, 2000).

Further problems arise in the enormous importance of language in maths and the central role it plays in enabling children to understand its complexities. Numerous writers (Robbins, 2000; Staves, 2001; Paterson et al., 2006; Porter, 2010) have indicated that those in the SLD spectrum '*are very likely to be at a serious disadvantage in learning*' (Imray and Hinchcliffe, 2014, 170) because of their severe communication difficulties.

The OECD have defined mathematical literacy as

> an individual's ability to identify and understand the role that mathematics plays in the world, to make well founded judgments and to use and engage with mathematics in ways that meet the needs of that individual's life as a constructive, concerned and reflective citizen.
>
> (OECD, 2006, 1)

The key words here are the '*ability to identify and understand the role that mathematics plays in the world*' because the very act of identifying the role maths plays directly implies the ability to understand abstract concepts and the theory of maths. Those on the SLD spectrum are perfectly able to understand the practice of maths, because that is all around us and in everything we do. It is the theory of maths that confounds them. When, for example, children are involved in the simple process of shopping, they are automatically involved in learning about time, space, measure, shape, quantity, means of exchange, direction, money, speed, position, sequencing, counting, etc. It is not important that they know this, or that they are taught these things in a detailed, compartmentalised manner in order to deepen learning in each individual section of maths. It is important that they learn to shop for themselves and learn to shop as independently as they possibly can. And of course learning to shop brings in all sorts of other necessities for learning and highlights the holistic nature of a fit-for-purpose SLD curriculum model, since this also requires all sorts of other independence skills from dressing and undressing to travel training via cooking and food technology, not to mention keeping oneself safe, thinking and problem-solving, self-determination, self-confidence, social skills, and communication skills.

Learning to be literate

As with numeracy, so with literacy, which all children in the United Kingdom, whether they be in mainstream or special schools, spend an inordinate amount of time 'learning'. Literacy is generally, in both types of school, almost exclusively to do with reading and writing, even though we are faced with the same problems of achievement as are present in mathematics for those on the SLD spectrum. That is, by definition, the very highest levels anyone with SLD can be expected to achieve will still only be at the starting point of the curriculum. As a reminder, a learner working at P8 in reading will be expected to:

> understand that words, symbols and pictures convey meaning. They recognise or read a growing repertoire of familiar words or symbols, including their own names. They recognise at least half the letters of the alphabet by shape, name or sound. They associate sounds with patterns in rhymes, with syllables, and with words or symbols.
>
> (QCA, 2009, 11)

Even learners working at slightly above these levels (say within the beginnings of the UK National Curriculum) will hardly be further along the literacy journey, though, of course, the rote learning trap is just as problematic in reading as it is in number. Many with a dual diagnosis of SLD and ASD may well be able to read quite fluently, though not necessarily have any understanding of what they are reading (Imray and Hinchcliffe, 2014). Autism is the singular condition for observing the propensity for language and communication to go off in separate directions (Jordan, 2001). So by definition, all learners with SLD, no matter how much work is put in, no matter how many years spent studying, will only be able to achieve literacy to the level normally attained by neuro-typical, conventionally developing learners by the age of 6 or 7. And we must surely ask the question about whether this is a level worth attaining if that is as far as they can get? In an analysis of a number of studies from Burgoyne et al. (2012), Burgoyne et al. (2013), and Hulme et al. (2013) which collectively reported on a two-year longitudinal study set up to compare the progress made by a group of 49 Down's Syndrome (DS) children with a group of 57 typically developing (TD) children after extensive one-to-one tuition in phonic skills, Imray (2015) questioned the logic behind the findings. All of the reported studies found three prime factors which predicted progress in reading: namely (i) age (with younger children making more progress); (ii) language, with integrity of speech production, vocabulary knowledge, and, especially, receptive language being key (those with higher levels making more progress); and (iii) the number of intervention sessions children received (those receiving more intervention making more progress).

The studies are clear that the DS children, on average, make better progress using phonic teaching techniques than those who were taught in more conventional ways, given exactly the same amount of one-to-one instruction over the same amount of time. Two key points need to be noted however. Firstly, though the researchers were only concerned with Down's Syndrome and not SLD, the term Down's Syndrome covers a range of learning difficulties including severe and even occasionally profound, with most individuals with DS functioning in the mild to moderately impaired range of cognitive ability (Chapman, 2003). Secondly, both Burgoyne et al. (2013) and Hulme et al. (2013) reported on '*a very high degree of longitudinal stability in reading skills in children with DS*'. That is, children with DS, even those with mild or moderate learning difficulties, do not, on the whole, make much progress in reading over time. This is highly significant.

The facts are that in the Burgoyne et al (2013) study, the **average** improvement using specifically taught phonics was 4.5 additional words over a 20 week period of 1 to 1 instruction every day for 45 minutes. This compared to an average improvement of 2 additional words for those not receiving the instruction. Yes, this is better, but does it justify the time and staff allocation? Taking this as a whole year's work of 45 minutes a day and 1 to 1 instruction, we can expect 9 new words to be learned for the average DS child as opposed to 4 new words without the phonic specific instruction. We have already established that all of these children were being educated in mainstream schools and we must expect the average ability to be well above the P8/L1 of the high flyers in special schools, and still they will only make on average, 9 new words over a year.

(Imray, 2015, 9, original emphasis)

This is an inordinate amount of time and resources. What else could we do with this time and these resources, especially, for example, if we devoted this time to improving individual learner's abilities to communicate effectively (Grove, 2013)?

Further, all three studies remark on a consistent lack of significant improvement in decoding non-words amongst the DS population, irrespective of their ability levels, but much more markedly so at the lower intellectual levels. This is highly significant because it implies that phonic decoding skills are not established in this population and confirms the surmises made by previous studies (Roch and Jarrold, 2008, for example), which argued that DS children mainly use whole-word recognition techniques. The Burgoyne et al. and Hulme et al. studies do recognise this point but do not, perhaps, give it sufficient emphasis and it is entirely plausible that the DS children are using basic rote memory techniques without having the level of working memory required to be consistent in phonic blending as a generalised reading technique.

The point here is that teaching phonics to any learners who are working consistently and over time at or below level 1 of the UK National Curriculum is largely pointless. This is because whilst those with SLD may well attain a number of individual words of reading, they will never, by definition, become *functional* readers in any accepted sense of the word. They will, in effect, remain at the literacy levels expected for an average 5- or 6-year old and that is a very low literacy level indeed. This does not mean that we should not be teaching reading, but we should be confining our instruction to contextualising everyday words in everyday reading use by the individual children and young people concerned in the contexts in which they need these words.

It may therefore be of merit to take the view that if we as educators, form a rounded, collective and considered opinion that an individual pupil is highly unlikely to achieve above L1 of the National Curriculum (the levels typically achieved by a conventionally developing 6 year old) taking time in continuing to teach children to read is of itself, highly contentious.

(Imray, 2015, 11)

It is somewhat ironic that our obsession with the 'rights' of all children to be able to access a mainstream curriculum model might teach those on the SLD spectrum to read the word 'ice cream' without ever teaching the same learner the necessary skills to go out and independently buy one.

Defining the PMLD spectrum and the SLD spectrum[2]

Given that we are attempting to reach out beyond the shores of the United Kingdom, and given the problems associated with inclusion are undoubtedly universal, we believe it worthwhile attempting a unified and unifying understanding of the terms PMLD and SLD. We believe that our revised definitions below, give much-needed clarity and specificity to two groups of learners who have been educationally side-lined and ignored for far too long, and are the definitions we have used thus far and will continue to use throughout the book. We must emphasise that these descriptions constitute broad but defining learning characteristics that fit specific groups of learners. Any definitional discussion is bound to be blurred and less precise at the edges, and there are bound to be some learners who stretch the definition, but this does not mean that the definitions do not have value.

Pupils with profound and multiple learning difficulties (PMLD) are on a spectrum that indicates that they have profoundly complex learning needs. In addition to profound learning difficulties, pupils are likely, though not in all cases, to have other significant difficulties such as physical disabilities, sensory impairments, and/or severe medical conditions. Pupils require a high level of adult support, both for their learning needs and also for their personal care. They are likely to benefit from engagement across all senses and will need a curriculum which recognises that all learners will, to a greater or lesser degree, have difficulties with object permanence, contingency awareness, declarative communications, making choices, learning by imitation, and following instruction. Pupils generally communicate by facial expression, body language, and other non-verbal methods. They will be working academically, consistently, and over time within P-scale range P1-P3, perhaps reaching some elements of P4, throughout their whole school careers to the age of 19 and beyond.

Pupils with severe learning difficulties (SLD) are on a spectrum which indicates that they have significant intellectual and cognitive impairments and may also have difficulties in mobility and coordination. Pupils will to a greater or lesser degree have severe communication difficulties, which will affect both expressive and receptive communication skills. Other difficulties will be experienced to a greater or lesser degree in understanding abstract concepts, maintaining concentration and attention, retrieving both short-term and long-term memory, utilising sequential memory, exercising working memory, processing information, retrieving general knowledge, thinking, problem-solving, and generalising previously learned skills. They will be working academically, consistently, and over time within the P scale range P4-P8 for all of their school careers to the age of 19 and beyond, though some may reach into the opening levels of a neuro-typical academic curriculum such as the UK or Australian National Curriculums or a US Standards-Based Curriculum.

If we can reach agreement about which pupils may be regarded as falling within the SLD and PMLD spectrums, we may begin to explore the possibility of what we might be teaching them. First, however, the issue of why we might be teaching them must be addressed.

Notes

1 The odd 'barrier' here is *the ability to initiate proto-declarative communications*. There are two elements to this, since the ability is one thing, desire is another. It may be that for some, particularly those on the autistic spectrum, there is no desire, and the ability might well therefore be hidden.
2 We would very much like to acknowledge the input of members of the SLD Forum for their contributions to the formulations of these definitions.

5 The pedagogical imperative

Research, writing, and discussion around the pedagogy of PMLD and the pedagogy of SLD are almost entirely absent from academic considerations, having been completely swallowed up by the inclusionist agenda. This argues that *all* children learn across a continuum (Lewis and Norwich, 2005; Norwich, 2013) and, ipso facto, all children can, and indeed should, access the same curriculum. That there is no hard evidence, and indeed precious little soft evidence, to support this contention has not stopped inclusionists from asserting the 'rightness' of their cause. But whether one adopts a hard-line universalist view, or a more amelioratory, moderate line which acknowledges the potential role of specialists and special schools, we have taken the position that for inclusion as a term to make any sense, there has to be a clear consensus and understanding that inclusive education is a process of increasing participation and decreasing exclusion from the culture, community, and curricula of mainstream schools (Booth et al., 2000). Without this as a central tenet, any discussion around the issue becomes discussion about education, not inclusion.

What does the research tell us?

> Much of the debate in academic journals in the past decade around the education of children with SLD has been based on the assumption that the ideal to be aimed for is access to the same curriculum for all children, using broadly similar pedagogical strategies, differentiated only on the basis of the individual learner's responses.
>
> (Ware, 2014, 501)

Such an approach, argues Ware, is, however, not founded on evidential research since there is, in fact, very little evidential research, and certainly not enough to inform opinion, an echo of previous similar findings

(Pring, 2004; Porter, 2005b; Ware, 2005; Norwich, 2013). Further, and even more problematically, when the purpose of the research is to promote inclusive practice, it tends not to reflect what practitioners are experiencing in the classroom.

> The link between research and practice, academic debate and day to day life in the classroom often seems tenuous at best. . . . However much evidence is collected of the effectiveness of an intervention in a research setting, it will make little difference to learners with SLD unless we can also come to understand how effective interventions can be made sustainable in ordinary classrooms; research into this issue is critical.
>
> (Ware, 2014, 502)

As has been shown in Chapter 3, there is a strong and consistent disconnect between what inclusionist theorists and researchers suggest should happen and what practitioners are able to make happen.

Only half a pedagogy?

There has been some thought given to the pedagogy of special educational needs, but this has taken elements of a definition of pedagogy from Alexander (2004) that does not seem to address the (for us) key imperative of pedagogical thought; that is, why are we teaching what we're teaching? This is because for inclusionists, whether they be Cigman's (2007) universalists or moderates, the question is simply not addressed. The 'why are we teaching?' question is answered by equal rights arguments that all children have an equal right to education, and it is axiomatically assumed that the same curriculum model, or at least variations of (or different *approaches* to) the same model is the only morally appropriate option. Teaching a different, separate, specifically designed and 'special' curriculum to those with special educational needs, rather than teaching the same curriculum differently, would after all be marking such children out as fundamentally other, thereby labelling and possibly stigmatising such children (Hart et al., 2007; Gillard, 2009).

In the United Kingdom, Davis and Florian (2004), Rix et al. (2009), Florian (2009), Florian and Black-Hawkins (2011), and Hart and Drummond (2014), for example, all approach the question of pedagogy from a special educational needs perspective; that is, taking the whole of special educational needs as though there is some common pedagogic sense in doing this. Why? The only commonality of all the various and disparate groupings is that pupils within them are different enough from mainstream, neuro-typical, conventionally developing learners that such pupils require some additional thought and possibly additional resources for their disability not to become a handicap.

For Florian and Hegarty (2004)

> the term SEN covers an array of problems from those arising from particular impairments to those related to learning and behavioural difficulties experienced by some learners some of the time . . . Many people are disabled by an impairment but they may or may not be handicapped by the condition . . . However, there are some conditions and impairments that are known to create barriers to learning unless accommodations are made. A person with a visual impairment, for example, **may need some kind of support or accommodation to achieve the same functioning** as the person without the visual impairment. . . . The term special education is often used to refer to the process of making such accommodations.
>
> (quoted in Davis and Florian, 2004, 34, our emphasis)

Here the assumption is that, when appropriate accommodations are made, those with a visual impairment **can** achieve the same functioning, and from an academic, intellectual point of view that is of course entirely feasible, though we are not expert enough to judge. We can however categorically assert that for those on the PMLD and SLD spectrums there is **no possibility** of achieving the same functionings, irrespective of the level and degree of accommodations made. Learners on the PMLD spectrum will, by definition, only achieve, at the very best, to the level of P4 and learners on the SLD spectrum will, by definition, only achieve at the very best to levels which correlate to the very beginnings of the neuro-typical, conventionally developing curriculum model that is the UK National Curriculum (Ndaji and Tymms, 2009; Imray, 2013). There is no reason to believe that the situation is any different in the Australian National Curriculum or an American 'Standards-Based' Curriculum. There are therefore unasked (and equally unanswered) questions as to whether such achievements justify 17-plus years of full-time education.

Davis and Florian (2004) accept that

> this process of making accommodations does not constitute pedagogy but is an element of it. Our view is that questions about a separate special education pedagogy are unhelpful . . . and that the more important agenda is about how to develop a pedagogy that is inclusive of all learners.
>
> (p. 34)

Unfortunately, the studies following on from Davis's and Florian's (2004) paper that also seek to address the pedagogy of SEN, also adopt this position: '*questions about a separate education pedagogy are unhelpful*' and therefore we won't think about them! They are, therefore, effectively confining their findings to elements of what good teachers do to differentiate their teaching to those with special educational needs. We have no doubt that these are important issues, but they totally ignore the fact that as well as this, a key element of Alexander's definition of pedagogy is his contention that for a curriculum model to be effective, teachers need to consider

> the various ways of knowing, understanding, doing, creating, investigating and making sense **which it is desirable for children to encounter**, and how these are most appropriately translated and structured for teaching.
>
> (Alexander, 2004, 11, our emphasis)

And this is very much the key to such discussions; is it desirable for children with SLD and PMLD to encounter a neuro-typical, academic curriculum model? Why is it desirable that so much time, energy, and resources are spent on a model that doesn't work for the few, just because it works for the many?

Because of different definitions, it is often difficult to assume a commonality of understanding between other countries and the United Kingdom, which is one of the reasons why we have pressed for a common definition of the terms SLD and PMLD in Chapter 4. It may be, however, especially as so much of the debate is about outcomes, that American students with severe disabilities as, for example, described by Ayres et al. (2012) are at the high-functioning end of SLD, though the principles still apply. Their point about this relates directly to the pedagogical issues at the centre of this chapter. Why are we educating these learners? For Ayres et al. education is directly related to outcomes, what happens after education, that is, the purpose of education. Where, they ask, is the evidence that a standards-based curriculum (SBC) benefits students with severe disabilities? Those arguing for an inclusive single curriculum model need to conduct a careful examination on the outcomes for students with severe disabilities.

> Are they more likely to go to college? Are they more likely to get jobs after leaving school? Are they more likely to live independently? Are they more likely to participate in their communities in meaningful ways? Research on alternate assessment seems to stop dead and simply evaluating progress on SBC without making cogent links to post-school outcomes.
>
> (Ayres et al., 2012, 15)

Universal design for learning

Much has been made in the United States of Universal Design for Learning (UDL) as being a solution to curriculum design barriers for those with SEN, but again, the basic premise assumes a common curriculum. The UDL argument adopts the premise that all learning can be divided into three sets of neural networks: recognition (the 'what' of learning), strategic (the 'how' of learning), and affective (the 'why' of learning), which, though distinguishable from each other, work closely together to co-ordinate even simple acts.

> The principles of UDL enable us to recognize that variance across individuals is the norm, not the exception, wherever people are gathered. Therefore the curriculum should be adapted to individual differences rather than the other way around. In this sense, traditional curricula have the 'disability', because they only work for certain learners. They are filled with barriers that are erected at the point of curriculum design.
>
> (Hall et al., 2012, 4)

Two interesting points here. Firstly, the ways in which curriculum design can be altered so that it is '*adapted to individual differences*' bears remarkable similarities to the accommodations suggested by, amongst others, Davis and Florian (2004), Rix et al. (2009), Florian (2009), and Florian and Black-Hawkins (2011) noted above. The fundamental difference is that advocates of UDL (for example, Rose et al., 2005; Hall et al., 2012; Rose et al., 2014) argue for such accommodations to be built in to the curriculum at the point of design rather than added as an afterthought. But the accommodations suggested are not new, they are accommodations that experienced (and specialist) teachers of SLD and PMLD routinely use in special schools throughout the United Kingdom and which have been the stuff of sound research and practice for many years (McConkey and McEvoy, 1986; Nind and Hewett, 1988; Longhorn, 1988; Grove and Park, 1996; Coupe O'Kane and Goldbart, 1998; Lacey and Ouvrey, 1998; Staves, 2001; Aird, 2001; Ware, 2003; WAG, 2006; Imray and Hinchcliffe, 2014; Lacey et al., 2015 to name but a few). The suggestion is then that had, for example, the 2014 UK National Curriculum revisions taken account of the considerable amount of research and reporting on sound practice and built in the suggested accommodations, only some of which are noted above, the new National Curriculum would have become fit for purpose for all learners on the SLD and PMLD spectrums.

Unfortunately, this would not and indeed could not have been the case, because the start of the curriculum is still the start and learners on the

PMLD spectrum will not, by definition, ever reach anywhere near the start, whilst only a very few learners on the SLD spectrum will, by definition, ever reach levels that equate to even the very earliest levels and most will also not reach the start. Similar arguments have already been put within this 'same content' restriction, by McGuire et al. (2006) and Shakespeare (2006), arguing that UDL is not 'universal' at all, in that it cannot meet the needs of *all* learners.

And (our apologies about being boring about this) we would remind readers that this is not dependent on the quality of teaching or the degree of accommodations made or the high or low expectations of staff or the staffing levels applied or the resources used or whether they are being educated in 'inclusive' or 'segregated' settings. Low-quality teaching, inadequate teacher and teaching assistant (TA) expertise, poor understanding of the nature of SLD and PMLD, low and negative expectations of staff, poor resources will all probably result in a greater degree of failure, but all will inevitably fail. We are not saying, and never have said, that learners on the SLD and PMLD spectrums cannot learn; we are saying, and will continue to say, that all will struggle enormously with an academic curriculum model and the more firmly entrenched they are within the respective learning difficulty spectrums, the more monumental these struggles will be.

Florian, one of the United Kingdom's most vociferous exponents of the 'universalist' approach to inclusion regards the continued pedagogical problems as being three-fold. What is needed, she argues, is (i) clearer thinking about the fulfilment to the right of education, (ii) challenges to deterministic beliefs about ability, and (iii) a shift in focus away from education's 'bell-curve thinking' which concentrates on education's 'normative centre' and differences amongst learners and towards 'learning for all' (Florian, 2014).

Firstly, as Florian accepts, the right to education is surely not disputed by anyone, at least in First World economies. We have no doubt that this is an extreme challenge in many parts of the world, but readers must excuse us for believing that this might be the subject of another book and is not within the remit of this one. What is disputed is the right to the same education, because that doesn't make sense, any more than the right to the same education makes sense for 3-year olds, 13-year olds, and 23-year olds. These are very different educations, deriving from quite different pedagogies and delivering very different curriculums, yet they will be related to each other far more than curricula for those with SLD and PMLD compared to neuro-typical, conventional models. That is because neuro-typical, conventionally developing 3-year olds, 13-year olds, and 23-year olds can all be expected to pass through the same educational landmarks even though their journeys might have different destinations. The journey for those with SLD and

PMLD will be fundamentally different. Why are differences acceptable in age but not in children, young people, and adults who are consistently and over time working at developmental levels way outside of their chronological age?

Secondly, Florian may not like 'deterministic beliefs' but the UK National Curriculum experiment is very, very clear: children on the PMLD and SLD spectrums do not even reach the beginnings of the curriculum, never mind succeed within it. Denial of a fact does not alter the fact.

Thirdly, and similarly, not liking mathematical truths – there is a norm and there is a bell curve which indicates the broad parameters of that norm – does not alter the mathematical fact of the norm. Florian seems to accept the term 'special educational needs' but not the consequences of that truth, that 'special' is not normal. This in turn echoes the UDL philosophy that

> enables us to envision a time when there will be one curriculum that is designed to be truly appropriate for all learners. 'Universal' doesn't mean 'one-size-fits-all'. Rather, it means that all learners with all their individual differences have equal and fair access and opportunity to learn the **same content** in ways that work best for them.
>
> (Hall et al., 2012, 4 our emphasis)

And we come back to the key pedagogical question that is continually ignored: why should the content be the same when some learners consistently fail at mastering that content?

Differing the expectation whilst keeping the same content

The second interesting point relating to UDL also bears similarities to UK initiatives which have a long history, dating back to the very earliest attempts at making the UK National Curriculum accessible to those on the SLD and PMLD spectrums by essentially re-writing the National Curriculum subject areas to include developmental levels of achievement that occur before the beginning. In other words, if learners cannot reach the start, let's move the start to an earlier developmental level. So for example, Bovair et al. (1992) and Sebba et al. (1993) have published 'how to' guides and Nind (2005), Pease (2008), Rayner (2011), and Lawson and Byers (2015) have put forward similar arguments favouring the notion that the delivery of (national) curriculum subject areas ensures breadth and balance and a context for teaching which is universal. This approach however has two debilitating consequences.

Either, as Ware (1994) has pointed out

> the process involved is . . . one of examining the activities in which pupils are taking part in order to identify the [National Curriculum subject] content within them.
>
> (p. 71)

And/or, the reflection of the subject on offer becomes mere tokenism as teachers 'pretend' to be teaching subjects whilst trying to teach something else entirely. One can easily see how this can come about. Teaching a child to cross a road independently becomes geography; the curriculum emphasis being visiting and observing local landmarks. Trying to encourage a child's sequential memory of routine events previously experienced becomes history; the curriculum emphasis being on events in the past. Teaching a young person to communicate effectively with his peers becomes English, because communication can be related to language and that is where language resides, even though the learner may not in fact be using language. This might not be so problematic were it not for the huge amount of time and energy wasted by such duplicity, since we can be fairly sure that (teaching being what it is) detailed planning documents and proof of curriculum inclusion will be required. And what exactly is the point of such pretence? If it is merely to ensure breadth and balance, a key consideration for many UK inclusionists (Rayner, 2011; Lawson and Byers, 2015) as well as American ones (Courtade et al., 2012 for example), this is breadth and balance by illusion.

Accepting the need for specialism whilst keeping the same content

We have spent much time in this chapter analysing the views of universalists, but what of the moderate's position? Is it fundamentally different? On first glance it appears to be, particularly in their recognition and acceptance of specialist teaching that may take place, in whole or in part, away from the mainstream classroom (Cigman, 2007; Hornby, 2015 for example). Norwich (2013) posits that

> as a concept and practice it [universalism] is based on false dichotomies. Extending what is available in the general class can be seen as extending/adding to generic teaching for some children. Assuming that all children can learn and their learning abilities can change is compatible with recognising learning dispositions. Recognising limits to learning also does not mean that limits are necessarily fixed.
>
> (pp. 159/160)

And this is true; limits to learning are not necessarily fixed, for most learners, and perhaps even for all learners. But learning to what end? Learning that can be established even with specialist teaching, when working within a pedagogy designed for neuro-typical, conventionally developing learners, only reaches the very beginnings for even the most successful learners with SLD. Mastery cannot, by definition, no matter how able the learner with SLD and PMLD, be achieved. The near-30-year experiment that is the UK National Curriculum tells us this is so.

For Norwich, the relationship between pedagogy and curriculum is answered in finding a balance in the different options for curriculum design in terms of curriculum commonality and differentiation, a position we shall look at in the next chapter. However, what is not addressed, yet again, is whether the moderate position he espouses (specialist teaching/same curriculum) is worth the effort.

Conclusion

We do not see it as our role or our business to pontificate on matters relating to mainstream education, other than to note that the market-led pedagogy which pervades Western education is a shallow and false premise (Robinson and Aronica, 2015). The pedagogy of formal mainstream education in First World economies seems to be entirely related to the perception that examination success will provide a workforce suited to the twenty-first century, and the whole curriculum and the delivery of the curriculum is geared to this one end. As such they all have literacy and numeracy at the very centre of education, these being seen as strong indicators of a successful education system. In the United Kingdom,

the national curriculum for mathematics aims to ensure that all pupils:

- become **fluent** in the fundamentals of mathematics, including thorough, varied and frequent practice with increasingly complex problems over time, so that pupils develop conceptual understanding and the ability to recall and apply knowledge rapidly and accurately.
- **reason mathematically** by following a line of enquiry, conjecturing relationships and generalisations, and developing an argument, justification or proof using mathematical language
- can **solve problems** by applying their mathematics to a variety of routine and non-routine problems with increasing sophistication, including breaking down problems into a series of simpler steps and persevering in seeking solutions.

(DfE, 2013, 108, original emphasis)

Note the emphasis of *all* pupils achieving mathematical fluency, reasoning mathematically, using mathematical language, and solving problems by application of mathematical reasoning. This echoes the demands for all achieving literacy as well as the 'all means all' debate in the United States, the insistence of one national curriculum for all in Australia, and the fiction of full inclusion for all in Italy. The pedagogical reasoning of such demands are clear. 'All' does not mean learners on the SLD and PMLD spectrums, since such learners cannot, by definition, achieve such academic heights. Other groups may also be excluded by their learning difficulties, that is not for us to judge, but inclusion can have no meaning if two small but significant groups of children are axiomatically and, by definition, excluded from achievement.

What they can achieve is discussed in the next chapter '*The curriculum imperative*'.

6 The curriculum imperative

In the last chapter we commented on the paucity of research into the education of those on the SLD and PMLD spectrums, but one incredibly interesting longitudinal study, which might be entitled '*Can learners on the SLD and PMLD spectrums succeed within the common curriculum framework that is the UK National Curriculum?*' and which has effectively been running between 1988 and the date of publication, has delivered a resounding answer. No, they cannot. And the remarkable part of this study is that this piece of news seemingly comes as an enormous surprise to so many people, though thankfully not all.

> Because public education must serve all children's educational needs, the largest part of general education must be designed for the modal (most frequently occurring) characteristics of students and teachers.
>
> (Kauffman, 2002, 258)

But this modal model, however necessary, however fit for purpose, however well funded, however pedagogically sound, cannot fit everyone, because it is exactly that – modal.

> By definition, exceptional students require an extraordinary response from educators – something different from the ordinary, even if the ordinary is good. . . . Failure to create these explicit structures to accommodate students at the extremes of performance distribution inevitably results in their neglect. They are forgotten. They don't just fail a little. They fail a lot, and their noses are rubbed in their failures.
>
> (Kauffman, 2002, 259)

And learners on the SLD and PMLD spectrums continue to fail because they cannot, by definition, achieve at levels that go beyond the very beginnings of the curriculum they are supposed to be studying. Let us again be very, very clear on this; children, young people, and adults with severe or profound learning difficulties will not succeed in the National Curriculum, or indeed, in any curriculum model designed for neuro-typical, conventionally developing learners. They will not succeed because they have severe or profound learning difficulties. It is not possible for them to succeed. If they could succeed, they wouldn't have severe or profound learning difficulties. And *'they don't just fail a little. They fail a lot.'*

A curriculum model for learners on the SLD and PMLD spectrums will have key pedagogical directions of travel that will not be sufficiently compatible to a model designed for neuro-typical, conventionally developing learners, rendering irrational the expectations that both will be able to be delivered in a single classroom. Withdrawal to allow certain children to engage in learning the same curriculum as other children (Norwich, 2008) is therefore not sufficient, since we are arguing that it is necessary to teach entirely different curricula based upon entirely different pedagogical frameworks. Indeed we might pose the same issue from a different perspective: would inclusionists support all children working on the same curriculum model if that model was specifically designed for learners with SLD and PMLD?

Swiss Cottage School (2014), a serially Ofsted-rated 'outstanding' UK special school, have argued very cogently that schools should provide Informal, Semi-formal, and Formal curriculum models to learners on the PMLD, SLD, and MLD spectrums. Taking these in P scale terms, they regard the Informal model as covering P1 to P4, Semi-formal as covering P4 to P8, and Formal as P8 plus and into the United Kingdom's National Curriculum. Imray and Hinchcliffe (2014) have suggested that the base curriculum for those with PMLD should comprise of the key areas of cognition, communication, physical, care, sensory, creative, and citizenship. These are not to be considered as 'subjects' to be taught in a compartmentalised manner, largely because those on the PMLD spectrum do not learn in a compartmentalised manner. Very similar areas of learning have been suggested by a number of 'outstanding' UK schools in their own curriculum models, such as Victoria School (2009), The Bridge School (2010), and Castle Wood School (2012).

Equals (2016a) have suggested that education for those on the SLD spectrum should work through nine 'avenues of learning', these avenues comprising of:

- Communication – not English (or German or French or Spanish or whatever is the language of the country) but being able to engage socially and positively with others through speech, sign, symbol, object of reference, and/or any other means. The emphasis is entirely on communication rather than literacy, because this is a priority for learning for those with SLD and PMLD.

- Independence – as in, for example, dressing and undressing, showering, teeth cleaning, travelling to known destinations, shopping, handling money, cooking, self-care, independent living, etc. Independence is a key area necessary to ensure mental health, purpose, self-esteem, and self-confidence (Lacey, 2009; Imray and Hinchcliffe, 2014). We must ensure that all learners with either SLD or PMLD become as independent as they can be irrespective of any physical or intellectual impairment.
- Thinking and problem-solving – a schema that is not discretely taught but runs through every other learning avenue and is a key necessity for the prevention of learned helplessness (Seligman, 1975) so common in those on the SLD and PMLD spectrums. This cannot be taught through maths, the traditional vehicle for problem-solving, because the nature of that subject automatically abstracts and decontextualises the problems that learners will face in reality and places intolerable strains on working memory and generalisations skills.
- Play and leisure – freely engaging with the idea of having fun and enjoyment. It is how we all learn, but it is immensely challenging for those on the SLD and PMLD spectrums because of all the difficulties that will be experienced in communication, thinking, flexibility, and memory. Play is the classic area which comes so easily to neuro-typical children; they don't need to learn to play when they come into formal schooling at the age of five or six, since they do it so well already. It can, however, take a lifetime of learning for many on the SLD and PMLD spectrums.

Equals have also suggested a number of other key curriculum components, which may well bear some similarity to a neuro-typical curriculum model (Equals, 2016a), though of course the curriculum content and the teaching of these avenues of learning will be vastly different. These are

- Creativity – particularly related to dance, drama, music, and art.
- Citizenship – behaviour and emotional well-being, work, the communities around us, sex and relationships, being a part of society rather than apart from it.
- ICT and social media – a fundamental technology for facilitating communication for those with SLD and PMLD in the twenty-first century.
- Physical well-being – looking after my body, physical exercise, healthy eating, healthy living, etc.

- The world about us – a general topic-based schema to act as a humanities base for the acquisition of knowledge and exploration of individual or collective interest.

It is entirely unnecessary, argues Equals, to equate these to national curriculum or standards-based subjects, since the bases for both areas of learning are non-relational. That is, those working on a common (national) curriculum, work on an academic and, of necessity, abstract understanding of compartmentalised subjects. Those working on the SLD 'avenues of learning' curriculum are working on a non-academic, holistic mixture of concrete skills and processed-based learning. As far as we are aware, Equals's Semiformal Curriculum model is the first attempt anywhere in the world to write detailed, all-age schemes of work specifically designed for learners on the SLD spectrum. Our view is that these would also be eminently suitable for many with moderate learning difficulties as well.

All this is, however, in direct contradiction to the Lewis and Norwich (2005), perhaps up-until-now, defining position that there is no research evidence to suggest that those with SLD and PMLD learn differently to other children. But it is a central point of this book that it is also true that there is no research evidence to suggest that those with SLD and PMLD *do not* learn differently to other children. Nonetheless, Lewis and Norwich are sufficiently convinced to opine that

> Practical pedagogies for those with special educational needs might look different from dominant mainstream pedagogy, but these are differences, we have argued, at the level of concrete programmes, materials and perhaps settings. They are not differences in the principles of curriculum design and pedagogic strategy.
>
> (Lewis and Norwich, 2005, 220)

This theme is carried on by Norwich (2013), who makes much of the necessity for a central common curriculum.

> Though concepts of inclusive curricula are opposed to a 'one size fits all' model, there is still a commitment to teaching a common curriculum by different means: by different strategies and learning materials and media. This idea of diversity within a unity is one of the central issues and challenges confronted from an inclusive perspective to curricula and teaching.
>
> (Norwich, 2013, 54)

Norwich conceptualises this 'diversity within a unity' in Table 6.1 below.

Table 6.1 Model of different options for curriculum design in terms of the balance between curriculum commonality and differentiation (from Norwich, 2013, 67)

Design Option	Principles	Programme Areas	Specific Programmes	Teaching
1	Common	Common	Common	Common
2	Common	Common	Common	Different
3	Common	Common	Different	Different
4	Common	Different	Different	Different
5	Different	Different	Different	Different

Interestingly, Norwich is unable to conceptualise design options 1 and 5 as being feasible.

> Neither of these design options is used or advocated in most international debates and decisions about curriculum as either politically desirable or socially viable.
>
> (Norwich, 2013, 67)

This stance is uncomfortably familiar, being redolent of Davis and Florian's (2004) take on pedagogy (see page 49) that discussions around real differences are '*unhelpful*' and therefore not worthy of further consideration. Perhaps the best take on the problem is, however, to regard this as a 'dilemma' recognised as a 'choice' between two unpalatable options.

> If children identified as having a disability (needing special education) are offered the same learning experience as other children, then they are likely to be denied the opportunity to have learning experiences relevant to their individual needs.
>
> If children identified as having a disability (needing special education) are NOT offered the same learning experience as other children, they are likely to be treated as a separate lower status group and be denied equal opportunities.
>
> (Norwich, 2013, 65, original emphasis)

There are two points of concern for the second option. Firstly, if anyone wishes to view separate educational opportunities as 'lower status', that is up to them. We cannot make people take a reasonable view, but their unreasonableness is not a pedagogical validation – as long as the state and society as a whole don't regard it as such, since this might affect funding. To date we do not see this as an issue in the United Kingdom at least, where every single child has a legal equal right to education, though we are not as cognisant of the potential fragility of special education in other Western liberal economies. Secondly, 'equal opportunities' to do what? Fail? Again, we see no political will from any political direction, even in these economically straightened times, which might lead us to the conclusion that equality of the *right* to education is itself in danger for those who need separate learning experiences. These are therefore both straw-man fallacies.

Nonetheless, we do accept that the dilemma is there and needs to be recognised. What we do about it and which choice we make will depend on very many factors, but the capabilities of the child has to be the key consideration. How can we ensure that the whole of the child's educational experience is focused upon making him the best he can be and do the best he can do?

There are perhaps two issues which need to be analysed further; that is, (i) are we certain that one curriculum model is better for the child than another and, (ii) when do we make this decision?

Options of curriculum model

Some learners, those who are at the edges of PMLD, may indeed be involved for some of their time with other curriculum models (that is, those suitable for the SLD spectrum) and those who are on the edges of the SLD spectrum may well dip into either PMLD models, MLD models, or indeed a model suitable for neuro-typical learners. The balance must depend on the abilities, capabilities, and functionings of the individual learner, since we have to ensure that their education has the potential to allow them to do the best that they can do and be the best that they can be (Nussbaum, 2011a).

When do we make decisions on which model to work on?

If we have Informal, Semi-formal, and Formal models running side by side, there seems no reason why individual learners should not work on elements of more than one model at any time in their school careers, should that be appropriate for the individual pupil. It would be difficult to envisage the three models working in a mainstream classroom, however, because the specialist knowledge and experience required to effectively run both informal and semi-formal models would be considerably beyond that which could be expected of a mainstream teacher at either primary (5 to 11) or secondary (11 to 18). In reality, most learners with SLD and PMLD will probably work mostly and for most of the time within one model or the other, and it seems not unreasonable to expect such a decision to be made between the ages of 8 and 11 years.

The Rochford Review (set up by the UK government to look at assessment for learners with SLD and PMLD) is interesting on their take on 'subject-specific learning'.

> There is a small number of pupils nationally whose learning difficulties mean that they will not be engaged in subject-based learning by the time they reach the end of key stage 1 or 2.
>
> (Rochford Review, 2016, 6)

The Review recognises that some learners are not best served by a linear, academic curriculum model such as the UK National Curriculum, but leaves it open to individual schools to make such a decision. This is a dilemma, but it cannot be a dilemma without a resolution, because time is of the essence. Equals (2016a) is very clear on the matter and says of travel training (TT), for example:

> Independent TT is very complicated to master and schools will therefore need to maximise the number of learning opportunities available. There is no logical reason why the processes outlined here cannot be started at KS1 *[5 to 7 years of age]* and possibly earlier. It is certainly not unreasonable to assume that TT will be an activity which all learners will need to practice several times during every single week of their whole school career.
>
> (Equals, 2016b, 1)

And again:

> Learners may need several tens and possibly several hundreds of opportunities to learn the same journey at the same time of the day using exactly the same route for it to become established and before we can bring in the variations necessary for the generalising of the skill.
>
> (Equals, 2016b, 2)

The point being that, certainly, we have to ensure that all learners are given the maximum amount of time to ensure that they can be the best that they can be and do the best that they can do, whichever curriculum model(s) is/ are selected. If we are to do this successfully, a curriculum for learners on the SLD and PMLD spectrums must be:

*   Openly concerned with the idea of taking a dilemmatic approach to curriculum provision;
*   Holistic – not compartmentalised;
*   Open to variation – not linear;

- Open to being personalised – not generic;
- Concrete and contextualised – not abstract;
- Concerned with process – not just product;
- Achievable – not idealistic;
- Embedded with the concepts of independence, fluency, maintenance, and generalisation;
- Open to narrowness (encompassing a specific and individualised focus) as well as, and sometimes rather than, balance and breadth;
- Open to the concept that the learning difficulties can be (and probably will be) defining;
- Concerned that curriculum time will be made available for social inclusion where there are no other required educational outcomes.

Let us take these one by one and subject them to further examination; for ease of explanation, we are primarily going to refer to how those on the SLD spectrum learn.

Openly concerned with the idea of taking a dilemmatic approach to curriculum provision

Of course it may be that it is possible, with consistent, very high-quality expert and experienced provision and much one-to-one and very small-group intensive teaching, to bring those on the SLD spectrum up to near the academic levels of their neuro-typical, conventionally developing peers. What is obvious so far is that no educational system has yet been found to achieve this. Throughout the lifetime of the National Curriculum in the United Kingdom, those on the SLD and PMLD spectrums, who are working consistently and over time within levels at and below the start of the National Curriculum, have remained there for all of their school lives, that is, up to the age of 19 (Ndaji and Tymms, 2009; Imray, 2013a). Norwich (2008) is therefore right in his suggestion that the education system and, by association, the whole of society, is faced with a real dilemma. There has however *'been a notable lack of interest in the analysis of educational matters from the perspective of dilemmas'* (Norwich, 2008, 3)

Norwich speculates on the reasons behind this. Firstly, this may be because some regard the dilemma (in this case academic inclusion) as already resolved and certainly there is an overwhelming sense in academic journals and other published material that no right-thinking person could possibly argue against inclusion (Florian, 1998, Thomas and O'Hanlon, 2005, Boyle and Topping, 2012, Ainscow, 2016, for example). We are not suggesting here that these writers regard their countries' educational inclusion as being complete, they certainly do not, merely that the rightness of their case is automatically built into '*the tragedy of exclusion*' (Slee, 2012). Secondly, Norwich points out that the term 'dilemma' refers to '*alternatives which are unfavourable*' and which do not have definitive solutions.

> Their resolution involves some balancing, perhaps some compromise and therefore some giving up or loss of valued principles or outcomes.
>
> (Slee, 2012, 3)

Nor is it sufficient to rest on the argument that all learners have an entitlement, in an equitable, egalitarian sense to a particular curriculum model, or possibly certain base elements of a unified curriculum. Lawson and Byers (2015) note that entitlement expectations with regard to the UK National Curriculum have receded over the 27 years of its existence. The initial introduction in 1989 saw the UK National Curriculum being prescriptive and the 'right' to receive it an entitlement that automatically applied to all. It is an interesting interpretation of 'right' as obligation which cannot be refused! The 2014 version relaxes this prescription considerably so that, for example, at Key Stage 4 (14 to 16 years old) learners have a '*statutory entitlement to be able to study a subject*' in each of the four areas of arts, design and technology, humanities, and modern foreign languages (DfE, 2013, 7). Why?

It is typical of the absolute absence of any reflection on the nature of learning for those with SLD and PMLD that such a statement is made. Why modern foreign languages rather than any other subject? What logic does this carry for those on the SLD and PMLD spectrums who need all the time they can get learning to effectively communicate in English? Lawson and Byers (2015) point out the statutory differences with the 1989 model for all learners, in that in the latest version 'they are not *required* to study these areas but they *must have the opportunity* to be able to do so' (p. 241, original emphasis). But again, why? There is no attempt to fit such a statement into a reasoned pedagogical argument, because for these writers, there are no reasoned pedagogical arguments for learners with SLD and PMLD which mark them out as fundamentally different learners. We, however, would concur with the view that whilst all learners must have an entitlement to a curriculum that is fit for purpose and meets their specific needs, there is little benefit if they are included in structures which fail to do this (WAG, 2006).

As we have tried to suggest here, the nature and extreme complexity of both the severe and profound and multiple learning difficulty spectrums, as well as the absolute necessity of extensive repetition being built in to the learning process mitigates against fulfilling one's potential in *both* academic and alternative curriculum models. Choices have to be made, because not making such choices leaves insufficient time in the school life of the learner.

For us, the argument is made by the fact that, by definition, the very best that can be achieved by the most able on the SLD spectrum (that is, fulfilling their potential) is equivalent to the start of the academic model, and for most on the SLD spectrum and all on the PMLD spectrum, well below the start. Why would anyone make such a choice when so much can be achieved through a non-academic model?

This also opens up another debate about the relevance of neuro-typical (mainstream) time frames. There is some logic to seeing the validity of a curriculum framework as being in its ability to prepare the learner for the next stage, whatever that might be. In UK mainstream terms, there is a fairly seamless transition from 3 to 5 (early years), from 5 to 11 (primary), from 11 to 16 (secondary), from 16 to 18 (sixth-form), from 18 to 21 (university), and then on to work. Each curriculum model builds on and extends from the last.

These time frames however do not make sense and therefore cannot apply to those on the SLD or PMLD spectrums because of the degree of repetition required, the difficulties with communication and cognition, and the naturally extended time required for progress to be established within independence, fluency, maintenance, and generalisation, even within a specific SLD or PMLD curriculum model. For these learners the key ages are 2 or 3, when they enter the education system, and 19, when they leave it. It is not an accident that the majority of UK special schools specifically for those with SLD and PMLD cater for the 2 to 19 age range, and see this as a perfectly normal and sensible arrangement. For learners on the SLD spectrum, there may be some logic in delivering a broadly academic framework, particularly within literacy and numeracy, until the age of 8 or so, because this would allow sufficient time (i) to assess the accuracy of an SLD or PMLD 'diagnosis' and (ii) to make a reasonable judgement on academic potential. A reasoned, informed, experienced, and expert multi-disciplinary judgement can then be made (which will of course, include parents) and, if it is decided that a non-academic route is more appropriate, still leave 10 or 11 years to concentrate on a specialised SLD or PMLD curriculum model.

Holistic – not compartmentalised

The compartmentalisation of learning as structured within a mainstream curriculum model is of major concern, since compartmentalisation requires feats from the working memory that are generally, and as a rule, beyond those on the SLD and PMLD spectrums. In a neuro-typical curriculum model, all knowledge is compartmentalised into subject areas, and these are also further compartmentalised into, for example, reading, writing, speaking, and listening for English and numeracy, geometry, statistics, and algebra for maths.

The logical assumption is that deep and meaningful learning can only take place if we spend sufficient time in each compartment, so that when problems arise which require us to use our analytical skills, each child can synthesise their compartmentalised (specialist) knowledge and come up with at least one and, more likely, several possible potential solutions. However, this becomes a nonsense when a child with SLD delves into his compartmentalised learning to arrive at the shallowest of rote learned responses. When 80% of a group (those with SLD) cannot count and are not secure in number (Porter, 2000), there must arise a real question regarding the value of teaching maths in a compartmentalised manner. When 100% of a group (those with PMLD) cannot count, any concept of working on maths at any level is rendered ridiculous.

Given the defining learning characteristics and (mostly insurmountable) barriers to academic learning experienced by those on the SLD and PMLD spectrums outlined in Chapter 4, especially in the areas of communication, abstraction, working memory, thinking, and problem-solving and generalisation, it is undoubtedly questionable whether any compartmentalised teaching is of value. The recognition and lauding of '*more inclusive curriculum models*' having the ability to '*provide opportunities to gain key cross-curricula skills*' (Lawson and Byers, 2015, 242) is of little value if such cross-curricula skills are taught in a compartmentalised manner.

Open to variation – not linear

The UK National Curriculum, and virtually all similar neuro-typical, conventionally developing models such as the Australian National Curriculum and the US Standards-based Curriculums, are based around a linear, or building-blocks, model of learning (Hewett, 2006; Kelly, 2009). Children are taught one concept, the learning of which is established with time and repetition, before moving onto the next step, the understanding of which usually depends upon the firm establishment of the previous block. Numeracy is a classic example of this approach, where number moves to addition, and then through subtraction, multiplication, division, fractions, etc. It is not possible to move onto addition, the second block, if number, the first block, has not been established.

In the only such research we have been able to find, Porter set out to test whether pupils and students with SLD followed Gelman's and Gallistel's (1978) five counting principles by testing a large sample of 58 pupils between the ages of 7 and 14 on their ability to spot very simple errors within the counting process. She discovered that 80% could not (cited in Porter, 2000) but posited that this was because the special school attended by the 58 pupils did not take maths seriously enough.

Two points here; firstly, even if this was true, it seems extraordinary that the research was not repeated and, secondly, we do not personally know of any staff in any special (SLD) school in England and Wales who are surprised by this result; we only know of staff who are surprised that 20% of their pupils are secure in number. Many will be able to rote count, but this does not equal number security. Our own extensive experience leads us to support Porter's view that *at least* 80% of children in any SLD special school will not be secure in number and therefore innumerate, and this is despite very many of these schools spending considerable amounts of time and resources on numeracy teaching. This is also despite the fact that 92% of England's special school were rated as either good or outstanding in 2015 (38% outstanding) with only 8% requiring improvement (Ofsted, 2015). Clearly, the problem cannot be related to the quality of the teaching. When the only model available to teach maths is the linear (national curriculum) model, schools are bound to be presented with real difficulties and, inevitably, failure. Similar problems exist in the teaching of literacy, especially both reading and writing, again, both generally presented in linear terms.

Open to personalisation – not generic

Carpenter et al. (2015) are persuasive in their assertion that the twenty-first-century complexities presented by children and young people with learning difficulties are more severe and more diverse as medical advances ensure foetal survival. Such complexities will inevitably lead to spiky educational profiles demanding a degree of personalisation not previously thought necessary. Within a special school setting, it is entirely possible that a school housing 100 pupils will effectively have 100 curriculums. There are bound to be commonalities within these, especially within the deep and specialist knowledge required on the nature of the SLD and PMLD spectrums, but the essential necessity to regard each learner as unique remains.

But we wish to go further. Since we believe that those on the SLD and PMLD spectrums require a different curriculum content, it might appear that we cannot accept Universal Design for Learning (UDL), but this is not so. UDL argues that variance across individuals is the norm, not the exception, and therefore the curriculum has to be adapted for individual variation, not the other way around. We accept this for those on the SLD spectrum and for those on the PMLD spectrum. That is, whilst all learners on the SLD spectrum have commonality (they all have SLD), not all learners on the SLD spectrum are the same. The curriculum must therefore be able to carry variation, and sometimes this variation might be considerable, but the curriculum *content* is the same, that is the sameness is simply its applicability to all learners on the SLD spectrum.

Concrete and contextualised – not abstract

The abstraction of learning takes place almost as a matter of course throughout the National Curriculum; it has to, in order to house the huge amounts of information needed. But the ability to successfully deal with and understand abstraction is, again, generally outside of the scope and intellectual ability of those with SLD (Lacey, 2009; Imray and Hinchcliffe, 2014) and always outside the intellectual scope of those with PMLD (Aird, 2001; Imray and Hinchcliffe, 2014). Skills that arise from the ability to abstract (such as thinking, problem-solving, and generalising) need to be taught specifically in a very concrete way so that the learning is always contextualised. So, for example, discussing the weather in a classroom might seem a perfectly reasonable activity, but in an SLD class will probably only lead to rote responses. Children will learn, when asked '*What's the weather like today?*', to respond in a limited number of ways and they probably have a 33% chance of success; that is, in the United Kingdom, it is likely to be a) sunny, b) cloudy, or c) rainy. If the child consistently picks 'cloudy', the chance of success probably goes up to 90%!

The whole nature of abstraction is particularly pernicious in language, where we, as teachers, constantly use abstract language in our teaching. Take, for example, the fairly simple concept of big and small, and by extension big, bigger, biggest, or small, smaller, smallest. We may introduce the concept of big and small by comparing two familiar objects, let us say teddy bears or dolls; what we tend to forget, however, is that the words 'big' and 'small' are entirely abstract words. That is, their meaning is held in our ability to automatically generalise our understanding across a wide range of teddy bears and dolls.

This is already self-evident for the 6-year-old neuro-typical learner who is able to visualise the possibility of a very large teddy bear and a very small doll, even if they're not there in front of her, but is likely to be *much* more problematic for those on the SLD spectrum. And then of course the words big and small have so many variable options. The smallest doll can become the biggest doll if we stand her up; the smallest teddy can become the biggest if we put it right in front of our eyes; the biggest teddy is not the same as THE biggest teddy. For neuro-typical learners, the natural abstractions of language can be sources of fun and joy and creation through poetry and story-telling and drama; this can also be the case for those on the SLD and PMLD spectrums (Park, 2010; Grove 2014), but the joy and creation will come about much more through playing games, exploring relationships, learning about communication through play, just having fun, and much less from the lexicological nuances.

Then there is the whole issue of why someone on the SLD spectrum needs to know about the weather or the relative values of big and small, and this surely lies in what meaning these words are likely to have. The nature of the weather is only of concern if one is going to be out in it. 'Weather', as a word, is totally abstract and only becomes concrete when choices about appropriate attire need to be made. 'What's the weather like today?' may be a social gambit, but it is also fundamental to making choices about clothing. Similarly, 'big' and 'small' only attain concrete status when the words are given individual meaning based on the prospect of a child needing to make such a choice. If the child needs to understand concept of bigness to make choices about whether clothes fit or not, the child will need many opportunities to try clothes on, and it is preferable that at least some of these take place in a clothes shop. Similarly with bowls for breakfast cereal, or ice creams, or hats; all might need meanings of the words big and small applied to them and them alone. The learner may eventually understand how to generalise these meanings, but equally, the learner may not, and if not, at least we have concrete contextualised understandings.

Concerned with process – not just product

The consequence of our obsession with both SMART (Specific Measurable Achievable, Realistic, Time-bound) targets and hitting predicted outcomes is a pressure on the teacher to promote rote learned responses in order to fulfil the prediction and tick the necessary box (Riddick, 2009). This might be hitting the target but it is certainly missing the point. Learning for those on the SLD spectrum will be holistic in nature and as much about process as product. For those on the PMLD spectrum, it is virtually exclusively about process over product (Imray and Hinchcliffe, 2014). The focus on product is likely to lead to a lowering of expectation, since the focus on the target risks all sorts of incidental and accidental learning being missed (Imray, 2013b). In practice, learning will take place at the learner's pace, not the teacher's, rather like play with very young babies. We cannot instruct a baby to play, but we can facilitate opportunities for doing so. We cannot predict when a baby will reach a particular milestone, we can merely watch out for it and record it, if and when it happens. This is the nature of play as a process.

The ubiquitous nature of individual education plans (IEP) or variations on the theme of setting specific, narrow, individual targets for learners, so much part of special education for so very long, also of course militates against a process-based approach.

> Planning is considered to be about setting specific single learning objectives for which specific strategies are selected. There is no place for teaching which has multiple and related objectives which call for

inter-connected strategies. Neither is there a place for general teaching strategies where there are open-ended objectives.

(Corbett and Norwich, 2005, 22)

As long as curriculum initiatives are based on normative development, artificial and irrelevant milestones will be marked up as key to the development of the child. This is evident in all UK National Curriculum subjects, but particularly in English and maths and even more particularly in numeracy and literacy. So, for example, much is made of mark making as a milestone towards independent writing, but time spent within this milestone is only time well spent if predicted outcomes can reasonably encompass the achievement of functional writing. When they cannot, time spent mark making as a useful activity (rather than, say, art as a creative activity) is time ill spent because it will lead to nothing.

This is also entirely irrespective of the time given over to the exercise because the key word here is '*functionally*' literate and numerate. The reality is that the level that can be achieved at the opening levels of the UK National Curriculum in literacy and numeracy – that is, the level achieved by a neuro-typical 5- or 6-year old – is very low indeed and may well not be worth achieving if this is at the expense of functional independence.

The idea that functional literacy and numeracy is achievable for all follows two entirely erroneous assumptions, namely (i) that is what is good for one is good for all and (ii) that those with SLD or PMD learn in the same way as those who develop intellectually in a neuro-typical and conventional manner, just slower.

Achievable – not idealistic

When looking at the nature of teaching phonics to children and young people (or old people for that matter) with severe learning difficulties, we are struck by the importance of repeatedly asking the key pedagogical questions: Why are we teaching this? What are we trying to achieve? Are we making a difference? The facts remain, and nearly 30 years of the UK National Curriculum clearly tells us, that pupils with SLD do not make progress above the beginning levels and the *vast* majority are working within levels well below the beginnings (Ndaji and Tymms, 2009; Imray, 2013a). This is not a contentious issue, since by definition, the *very* upper limit of academic achievement will be at levels at or below the start of the UK National Curriculum, when neuro-typical, conventionally developing children are expected to be achieving by the age of 6 (DfE, 2012).

When teachers in mainstream classes ask themselves the same questions, their reasoning will be guided by what the pupil can reasonably expect to achieve by the time s/he leaves school. With the neuro-typical child, there is a reasonable expectation that the pupil will achieve at least level 5/6 and quite possibly higher by the end of key stage 4 at 16 years of age. The educational programme that is the UK National Curriculum is designed with this in mind. It uses strategies such as phonics to enable pupils to decode unfamiliar words so that s/he can both spell and pronounce reasonably accurately. Such strategies then allow the learner to further research meanings and spellings in a dictionary, whether this is on-line or not. It allows the learner to further develop his/her reading and writing away from the classroom, and success encourages the learner to discover reading as a pleasurable activity that is of use for and of itself. Decoding strategies such as phonics become essential tools to learn at the introductory levels because there is a reasonable expectation that the learner will be able to use them functionally as they move through the levels and achieve the higher reaches.

The point here is that this is an entirely different form of reading to the reading that can be expected of someone who is still working at and below the introductory levels by the time they reach the end of KS 4 at 16 years of age. Reading at this level is about being confident within a limited range of very familiar words, not about decoding unfamiliar words. Such familiar words are likely to be very personalised, key information-carrying words and are learned through symbolic recognition. That is, the learner sees the word as a symbol (which of course it is) and is likely to learn it by repetitive exposure. Pupils with SLD will probably learn the symbol for toilet fairly easily because it is an iconic symbol (that is, the drawing reasonably accurately reflects a toilet), but they will also need to recognise the word 'toilet', or in America 'washroom' (or more accurately 'Toilet' or 'TOILET', and lavatory or Lavatory or LAVATORY, or 'Washroom' or WASHROOM', etc.) because these words are often used in public places to indicate where the toilets or washrooms are.

Recent research has suggested that phonics is a legitimate approach for those with Down's Syndrome and, by (unstated) extension, SLD (Burgoyne et al., 2012; Burgoyne et al., 2013; Hulme et al., 2013) running against arguments that children with SLD will be more successful with a whole-word recognition approach (Roach and Jarrold, 2008). This does, however, fail to pose the key question: What is the point? We have sympathy with primary school teachers teaching children on the SLD spectrum because they have to make judgements as to what their pupils might realistically achieve by the time they're 11. This can be a dilemma, because teachers naturally don't want to be seen to 'give up' on pupils who, it is argued, may go on to make remarkable progress at some future time. But the reality is that if the child has SLD, the child will not become literate in the sense of being able to read fluently no matter what programme is put in place and no matter how remarkable the progress. This is because s/he has SLD; that is, it is a definitional perspective. The upper limits of educational ambition remain at or below the starting point for neuro-typical children. Worse still, schools will continue to try because they don't want to be accused of having low ambition and the inevitable result of this continuing to try is that the pupil will continue to fail.

The system, which works for the majority of children through the UK National Curriculum, is destined to make failures of our children because it is not designed with SLD in mind. If a goal is not achievable, and being literate in the accepted sense of the word is, by definition, not achievable, then we should not waste time trying to achieve it. There are too many other important things to do, such as ensuring that the child is able to communicate in a wide variety of situations and with a wide variety of people. Such skills take a considerable amount of time and will only be compromised by teachers continuing to follow meaningless and irrelevant programmes of study. Educational inclusion is a laudable ideal and may well be both possible and beneficial to the child and society for some groups of children with SEND, but this principle does not apply to those with SLD or PMLD.

Embedded with the concepts of independence, fluency, maintenance, and generalisation

Recognising that learning (and therefore teaching) can never be a linear process for children and young people with SLD and PMLD, Sissons (2010) posited that four key principles must remain priorities for true (deep and meaningful) learning to have any chance of taking place. These are (i) reducing prompting, helping the learner to move from dependence to independence; (ii) improving fluency, so that learners move from having an approximate to an accurate mastery of a skill; (iii) ensuring maintenance, so that learners can over time move from an inconsistent and perhaps fractured ability towards greater consistency; and (iv) improving generalisation, so that learners are able to move from learning a skill in a single context to the application of that skill, or perhaps even a variation of it, in many contexts. These are the core principles of Mapping and Assessing Personal Progress (MAPP), an assessment schema that is becoming increasingly popular in UK special schools. All teaching of those with SLD, Sissons argues, must hold these core principles in mind at all times if learning is not to remain both shallow and superficial.

Such concepts also ensure that a broadly developmental curriculum model which starts at the beginning and carries through to the end need not be the linear process that the early stages of neuro-typical models tend to be, because Sissons's four concepts ensure that we are teaching with lateral progression clearly in mind from the very beginning and, indeed, right through the process for as far as the learner is able to achieve.

Open to narrowness (encompassing a specific and individualised focus) as well as, and sometimes rather than, breadth

The general requirement of the accepted wisdom of a broad and balanced curriculum may not be applicable for all children and young people with SLD or PMLD for all periods of time (Imray and Hinchcliffe, 2014). In fact the insistence on this may be the worst thing we can do for certain children at certain times. This is especially true of very young learners and those struggling to come to terms with social relationships, but it can apply to many on the SLD and PMLD spectrums and be relevant for considerable extended periods of time, sometimes lasting many years. It is entirely conceivable that a number of learners will be in a moment where it is essential for all school staff to focus on, for example, decreasing behavioural tensions or teaching a child how to communicate effectively. For some children and young people, these are not just priorities, they are essentials that cannot be diluted for the period of time it takes to establish necessary core learning.

Critics of this view, such as Lawson and Byers (2015), note that narrowing the curriculum will inevitably 'ignore opportunities' for other learning. We do not doubt that that is probable, but it can be balanced by recognising the dilemmatic approach. The dilemma is between two alternatives which are both unfavourable in an ideal world; but if the learner is not at present in an ideal world, decisions will have to be made. We do not suggest a permanent narrowing, but a temporary narrowing, though temporary may well be defined in years rather than days or weeks and may be an essential for the learner's well-being and long-term progress.

Open to the concept that learning difficulties can be (and probably will be) academically defining

The difficulty here is that such a statement has, up until now, generally been seen in negative, ableist, disabling, limiting, and discriminatory terms, where the only response necessary is to note that this is yet another hackneyed version of the vastly discredited medical model of disability. There is almost no agenda for such discussion because the opposite of inclusion is exclusion, and how can anyone seriously support such a notion.

We do not however seek to exclude those on the SLD and PMLD spectrums from the education system; we seek to exclude them from a centrally imposed, one-size-fits-all pedagogic and curriculum model that is unfit for purpose and does not meet the needs of any learner with SLD or PMLD. Such learners learn very, very differently from the neuro-typical model (and even very differently from other groupings within the SEND umbrella) and it is no more reasonable to place them in an inclusive mainstream classroom than to place neuro-typical learners in an SLD or PMLD classroom. It is not sufficient to suggest that teachers need to

> receive training in inclusive education, and in-service teachers . . . exposed to training through continuing professional development.
>
> (Sokal and Katz, 2015, 50)

Training in inclusive education is one thing; training in how to teach learners on the SLD and PMLD spectrums is quite another. Indeed the whole concept that specialist initial teacher training in SLD and PMLD in the United Kingdom is 'inappropriate' (ASCET, 1984, para 14), which still holds sway despite the recommendations of the Salt Review (Salt, 2010) and the Carter Review (2015), further cements our view that insufficient thought (and in most instances, no thought at all) has been given to the matter by those in charge of education policy.

> The closure of specialist ITT courses in the education of children with SLD and PMLD in the middle of the 1990's has, arguably, had a catastrophic effect on schools up and down the UK, where the supply of well-prepared teachers qualified to teach children with SLD and PMLD soon dried up.
>
> (Imray and Hinchcliffe, 2014, xii)

Concerned that curriculum time will be made available for social inclusion where there are no other required outcomes

All of the above does not of course mean that social inclusion is not highly desirable, though Norwich's dilemmatic approach will also be needed here because there are bound to be time constraints and questions of alternative possibilities. How much of the school week should be given over to social inclusion? Are mainstream schools (especially at secondary level) willing to devote the time in the face of academic and examination pressures? Will governmental standards organisations such as Ofsted and Estyn in England and Wales recognise the value of inclusion for its own sake? Will inclusion receive a capital 'I', thus recognising Inclusion as a 'subject' to be taught like any other in all educational settings?

Perhaps more importantly, the whole issue of both educational inclusion and social inclusion must be discussed and weighed by the whole of society in the same way as the whole of society takes responsibility for its views on race and gender (Nussbaum, 2007). The almost exclusive concentration on education as the fulcrum for expressing inclusive language has led to a considerable societal toleration of discrimination against those with SLD and PMLD, and a diminution of their lives and life prospects that many might regard as staggering.

Perhaps, also, as both Terzi (2010) and Reindal (2010) have suggested, we might move forward from the oft-emotive and ultimately sterile debate between medical and social models of education as being the only philosophical options we might have. Rather we might look instead at adopting a Capabilities Approach which might inform both education in particular and society in general and thereby enable those on the SLD and PMLD spectrums to be the best they can be and to do the best they can do.

7   The capabilities imperative

In the 1980s the economist Amartya Sen (1985, for example) wrote of the need to look afresh at the relationship between economic justice and economic success by allowing, encouraging, and supporting each economy and each individual within that economy to do the best that they can do and be the best that they can be. He termed this the Capabilities Approach. Such a model attracted the attention of American philosopher Martha Nussbaum, in that it could be equally applied to what she regarded as being the three unresolved issues neglected by existing theories of social justice. These are justice to non-human animals, extending justice to all world citizens, and justice to people with physical and/or mental impairments (Nussbaum, 2004). It is obviously the latter with which we are now concerned.

For Nussbaum the Capabilities Approach can be defined as

> an approach to comparative quality-of-life assessments and to theorizing about basic social justice. It holds that the key questions to ask, when comparing societies and assessing them for their basic decency or justice, is 'What is each person able to do and to be?' In other words the approach takes **each person as an end**, asking not just about the total or average well-being but about the opportunities available to each person. It is **focused on choice or freedom**, holding that the crucial good societies should be promoting for their people is a set of opportunities, or substantial freedoms, which people then may or may not exercise in action: the choice is theirs. It thus commits itself to respect for people's powers of self-definition.
>
> (Nussbaum, 2011a, 18, original emphasis)

These emphases on (i) taking each person as an end, (ii) focusing on choice and freedom, and (iii) respecting people's powers of self-definition need to be explored further.

Taking each person as an end

It is really important to note that capabilities are not abilities or skills per se, which are described as *internal capabilities*, but rather the potential to make the most of them if actively encouraged and not debarred from doing so. Nussbaum refers to these as substantial freedoms or '*combined capabilities*', defined as

> not just the abilities residing inside a person but also the freedoms or opportunities created by a combination of personal abilities and the political, social and economic environment.
>
> (Nussbaum, 2011a, 20)

The fact that these are individually accrued leads us to an individual response rather than a collective 'disability awareness' where the individual is subsumed in a collective check-list of rights and benefits. '*Capabilities . . . are those actions and approaches to living that one values*' (Reindal, 2010, 5). Because capability frameworks are focused on what each person is able to do and to be, no minimum threshold of basic capabilities is required and no one is excluded on grounds of cognitive impairment from the responsibilities of societies to facilitate the individual exercise of combined capabilities (Nussbaum, 2011a; Wolff and de Shallit (2007)). Inbuilt into this is the recognition that those in control of the political, social, and economic environment have it within their power to enhance or impair. A 'decent' society is one which not only maximises the individual's potential for developing their internal capabilities, but sets up its institutions to maximise the individual's opportunities for exercising them, that is, *functioning*.

Focusing on choice and freedom

Functioning is key to the Capabilities Approach because it implies both the full ability to do something one is capable of doing and to be someone one is capable of being, but also not doing or being these things if the individual so (freely) chooses. Nussbaum (2011a) uses an example of Sens's comparing a person who is starving with a person who is fasting. Both have the same type of functioning where nutrition is concerned, but they do not have the same capability, because the person who fasts can choose not to fast, but the starving person has no choice.

How are we to regard functioning for those with severe and profound learning difficulties who may be deemed unable to make a choice because their cognitive abilities and reason can be called into question? When considerations of care, ethics, autonomy, and agency are so directly inter-related

(Rogers, 2016), issues of 'voicelessness' (Niemayer, 2014) may lead us to substitute our voice for theirs because judgements on whether self-determination is possible are so difficult.

Some readers of this book might have been quick to bracket the authors as purveyors of a medical model who see the difficulty residing in the person, arguers for a ceiling of achievement and a dampening down of ambition and horizon, because we have already pre-determined their ability, disabled them, and even, in the words of Goodley et al. (2015), rendered the child 'dis-human'. Certainly, we have consistently argued that those on the SLD and PMLD spectrums find learning extremely difficult and there are certain things they cannot, by definition do, in the same way as someone who is cortically blind cannot, by definition, see. It is, further, incredibly important that educators know this, but knowing what they (both educators and children) can't do is only part of the conundrum; knowing what they can do and perhaps even more importantly knowing what children *want* to do and *want* to be could be key. Want does not, however, equal ability, and ability does not necessarily equal capability.

Hollingsworth (2013), in the context of the justice system, maintains that it is important to recognise the way in which children's autonomy differs from that of adults: this could have implications for those who may not be considered to have agency. Reference to a Capabilities Approach suggests that children should be seen as 'becomings', with adults ensuring that decisions made during childhood do not have adverse future consequences. But 'becomings' implies a growth towards fully fledged being; when do those with PMLD and SLD become a being rather than a becoming? There exists a clear objective standard when children will become adults: it's called time, and the age of 18 determines that we can accept their being, their ability to make their own choices, their agency, whether this is acceptable to society or not and whether this has adverse consequences or not. This is not the case for those with learning difficulties. Here we see society's role as protecting; not just protecting the person from potentially illogical, harmful, self-destructive choices, but also, of course, protecting society from the consequences of such potentially illogical, harmful, self-destructive choices.

Johnson and Walmsley (2010) argue that dominant discourses in the wider community on what it means to lead a good life tend to exclude people with learning difficulties because the centrality of reason has historically defined what we mean by a good life. If people, because of their learning difficulties, cannot make decisions because they are (like a child) likely to make the wrong decision, how can we include them in the debate? We can care (for them) but not include. But whose reason are we interested in exploring? Reason is not seen as equal.

This might be considered to be an issue of fundamental freedom and it is here that Sen (1992) considers inequalities most pervasive. Terzi (2010) argues that since functionings are necessary for well-being and capability represents the various combinations of functionings which a person may achieve, restrictions to functionings represents 'vertical inequalities' and as such are matters of justice. Reindal (2010) also sees it as central:

> We may insist, then, that interpreting capabilities as opportunities to live a valued life and the life of one's choices is fundamental to human agency. While Sen has not employed the term 'empowerment', it closely relates to an enhancement of human agency, which is at the core of the capability approach as the capability approach *[emphases]* the possibility of freedom a person has to lead one kind of life or another.
>
> (Reindal, 2010, 5)

For Nussbaum this is a matter of dignity, where the

> conception (is) of the person as a social animal, whose dignity does not derive from an idealized rationality.
>
> (Nussbaum, 2007, 99)

And though she recognises the word as an '*intuitive notion*' (Nussbaum, 2011a, 29), it is one which she feels has a common understanding and meaning.

> The court cases that opened the public schools to *[people with severe cognitive disabilities]* used, at crucial junctures, the notion of dignity: we do not treat a child with Down syndrome in a manner commensurate with that child's dignity if we fail to develop the child's powers of mind through suitable education. In a wide range of areas, moreover, a focus on dignity will dictate policy choices that protect and support agency, rather than choices which infantilize people and treat them as passive recipients of benefit.
>
> (Nussbaum, 2011a, 30)

Respecting people's powers of self-definition

Imray et al. (in print) have conducted a piece of action research describing 12 months in the educational lives of seven students attending St Ann's School in west London, a secondary (11 to 19) special school with some 91 students on role. Of these students, 32 are on the PMLD spectrum and 59 are on the SLD spectrum (that is, their learning characteristics fall within the definitions to be found on page 45) whilst 37 also have an additional diagnosis of autism.

St Ann's (judged by Ofsted to be a good school) is rightly proud of the fact that they have only issued one fixed-term exclusion in the last 15 years, have never rejected a potential student on the grounds of behaviour, and, fairly typically for a UK special school, operate an eclectic positive (that is, non-punitive) behaviour support policy. Despite this, the school was being consistently stretched in its ability to work with a number of young men who were not responding to what might be termed classic Positive Behaviour Support (PBS)-style interventions. Six of these seven were deemed SLD/ASD and one SLD, all functioning between P4 and P6, all displaying consistent and extreme challenging behaviours as daily occurrences. Typical of such behaviours were hitting, slapping, biting, scratching, hair pulling, kicking, nail gouging, spitting at both staff and classroom peers, refusal to engage with set tasks, climbing, running away. All were assigned dedicated and highly experienced one-to-one support staff in their classes; two students were assigned two-to-one; all had personalised behaviour support plans aimed at intervention before the behaviour happened, that is, they were proactive rather than reactive. Physical interventions, from staff to students, were kept to an absolute minimum and then only used to protect others and help the student in crisis to get to a safe space as quickly and as easily as possible.

The extremes of behaviour tended to be cyclical but regular and often on a daily basis, and were being 'managed', but it was clear that there was deep unhappiness from the learners, peers, staff, parents, etc. and it was very difficult to clearly ascertain a reason behind any of the underlying issues, other than a profound dis-engagement with the formal educational process. A decision was therefore made to put all seven students in one class and, on the basis that all seven responded consistently aversely to doing anything that they didn't want to do, all demand was taken away. That is, the learners were free to do anything or nothing, free to come and go as they pleased (there are two largish self-contained rooms and an enclosed outside play area but no locks on any doors), free to be on their own or work or not work with any of the 10 highly experienced members of staff assigned to the class. There was no enforced timetable, though opportunities to play and engage with others were consistently provided, and all order, structure, routine, and, most importantly, demand were taken away.

If we begin with the assumption that all behaviour has a function it follows that it is, in the school context, a professional responsibility on the part of adults to work out what a child's behaviour is communicating. This is the essential purpose of empathy and is a particular concern when working with children with significant difficulties with speech, language and communication.

(Crombie et al., 2014, 18)

Over the three terms (around 40 weeks) of the 'experiment', behaviours came tumbling down so that violent behaviours, of the type described above, which were both routine and daily occurrences for all seven students now represented only 0.78% of the weekly occurrences for the whole class. In a seven week, half term period 2048 individual 45 minute sessions were recorded; only 16 of which were deemed to involve crisis behaviours. The curriculum had been temporarily narrowed and peace and calm had broken out!

As if this wasn't enough, there appeared a remarkable correlation between reduced challenging behaviours and increased engagements involving positive, interactive communications, initially just with staff members, but latterly also with peers. Such positive interactions have extended to home, with a number of parents reporting significant positive changes to their children's abilities to interact, engage, and self-manage potential crises. Individuals' communicative abilities significantly increased, especially in the area of signing, with the vast majority of communications now being positive as opposed to the previous negative predominance (Imray et al., in print).

What lessons can we draw from such a study that might relate to voice, agency and a Capabilities Approach?

In the regular classroom, none of the seven students of St Ann's chose to get involved with the individualised and highly differentiated education that was on offer, and if they did so, they did so reluctantly and only because a considerable reward was offered to them. The regular classroom consisted generally of a teacher and two support staff to six or seven students, with at least one additional one-to-one member of staff allocated to each of the seven. The curriculum offered was based broadly on a National Curriculum model, but highly differentiated to take account of the level of learning difficulty at the school. The standard of teaching from both qualified teachers and Teaching Assistants (TAs) was uniformly good and often outstanding, but despite this, the complexity of need demonstrated by these seven students continued to perplex and confound. What was evident was that an entirely different approach was needed.

Given the belief from the school's leadership team that all behaviours are communications (Imray and Hewett, 2015), that all challenging behaviours are 'normal' for those with learning difficulties (Hewett, 1998), and that challenging behaviour represents '*coherently organized adaptive responses to challenging situations*' (Emerson, 2001, 3), the concept that the school had to listen to what the behaviours were telling them seemed to be irrefutable logic.

Taking the three basic elements of ability, capability, and functioning, the school recognised that all seven students had the ability to communicate, even though these communications were in behavioural form (none of the students used extended language), but they lacked capability because the behaviours were almost all negative; that is, they communicated things which the learners didn't want to do or didn't want to be involved in. Further, positive communications were often compromised by the natural workings of the classroom, such as, now is the time for our 'good morning' session and next we'll be working on art, etc. Even when individual students worked on individual timetables, the essential work ethic of schools predicated against functioning, because the common wisdom of operating an educational establishment dictates that it is just not possible for individual pupils to decide what they want to do and when they want to do it all of the time, or more commonly, what they don't want to do and when they don't want to do it, especially if that means that they don't want to do anything!

Critics may argue that such a state of affairs indicates poor teaching, that the pedagogical 'how' of teaching (delineated by, for example, Florian and Black-Hawkins, 2011 and Hart and Drummond, 2014) needs to be revisited so that known teaching strategies can be applied to all learners; this charge is rejected by the school as a simplistic blanket answer. All seven students are part of what Carpenter et al. (2015) refer to as 'new generation children' with complex learning difficulties and disabilities (CLDD). These are children born in an age where huge medical advances have ensured that prematurity of birth is no longer an obstacle to survival.

> In the twenty-first century, children with CLDD are presenting with new profiles of learning needs that the teaching profession struggle to meet through existing teaching styles or curriculum frameworks. We need to be honest about this – for the sake of our professional practice, and, even more so, for the sake of the children.
>
> (Carpenter et al., 2015, 6)

These are children for whom we are '*pedagogically bereft*' (Carpenter, 2011). The common strategies, however well thought out, however well delivered, just do not work.

The Capabilities Approach does, however, offer us a real way forward provided we are able to take the risk and grasp the nettle. Because offering children the opportunity to decide upon their own education is a risk, it is diametrically opposed to the received wisdom that we know best, that we are in control, that children must learn like us and learn to be like us. The seven learners in St Ann's have demonstrated that if we are willing to be brave, to take risks, to open ourselves out to the possibility that all learners have agency and voice, a Capabilities Approach can work in education.

> It is difficult not to conclude that for people with intellectual disabilities (and other persistently marginalised groups) the conceptualisation and measurement of well-being should focus on well-being within a capability framework that views well-being as a function of life opportunities and achievements and whose measurement is best focused on the objective conditions in which people make choices and which shape their abilities to transform opportunities into their preferred ends.
>
> (Emerson and Hatton, 2013, 35)

However, such a policy has to be followed through into society as well if we are not to render capability into incapability once the learners leave school. It is entirely self-evident that there is a long way to go in education, but even further to go with society as a whole. We discuss this issue more fully in the next chapter.

8   The social imperative

In previous chapters we have seen that despite a great deal of inclusive rhetoric over the last 50 years or so, the full inclusion of learners with SLD and PMLD in mainstream educational settings has been problematised and opportunities have been limited. We have argued that instead of carrying on with the difficult assumption that these learners can be included in mainstream schools or access mainstream-type curricula in whatever setting, we need to ask why we teach what we teach when it comes to this sizeable group of learners. This may mean setting aside potentially unachievable ideologies, as well as finding a way of reconceptualising what an appropriate education for these young people might look like and, perhaps by extension, a more appropriate education for everybody.

In this chapter we will try to place these arguments within a wider social and democratic context, looking to the place of people on the SLD-PMLD continuum in society, how they are perceived by other people, and the values and understandings which underpin those perceptions. In doing so, we will advance the arguments put forward in the last chapter relating to a Capabilities Approach (Nussbaum, 2004, 2007, 2010, 2011a) as well as on Nussbaum's discussions of 'political liberalism', which seek to address issues of politics and social justice with respect to people with learning difficulties. We will also refer to Johnson's and Walmsley's (2010) analysis of 'a good life' for people with learning difficulties, which argues that adopting a Capabilities Approach encourages a re-imagining of social contracts and a reshaping of social roles and structures in order to create a truly inclusive democracy.

Nussbaum's (2007) contention that the most important thing society can do for people with learning difficulties is to support them in what '*they can do and be*' (p. 73) is often compromised by the fact that we may unconsciously '*project on them dominant norms from wider society*' (p. 128). Quite rightly we want them to achieve and to be happy in their lives, but at the same time we assume this achievement and happiness will reflect closely our own conceptions of what achievement and happiness looks like.

We see this commonly in media depictions of people with learning disabilities as being 'heroes' who somehow transcend their impairments to achieve in ways we can recognise from their non-disabled counterparts. It is only really when a disabled person is perceived to be escaping their condition and approaching what seems to be socially acceptable ways of 'doing' and 'being' that we are prepared to celebrate them. This was summed up in an article by Giula Rhodes in *The Guardian* newspaper on 10 September 2016 for which she interviewed John Williams about his autistic son. Williams said this:

> The thing is, we only really celebrate disability when there is a skill involved. Take the Paralympics, incredible as they are, they're all about strength, courage and bravery. All I really wanted to do was to celebrate the smallness of it all, of just being in the world without justification. There's joy in the little things.

'Being in the world without justification'. It's hard to think of a better phrase to describe what a good life might feel like for someone with SLD or PMLD, and in fact for all of us, and yet this is hard to achieve when policies and values, as Nussbaum (2007) reminds us, tend to be based on *'a single linear ranking of relative social positions'* (p. 141) within a society which *'shuns weakness and glorifies strength'* (O'Brien, 2016, 21).

Broderick and Ne'eman (2008), in an analysis of metaphors of disability, suggest that the language we use when we talk about disability points towards our own failure to acknowledge that people with disabilities have a full and equal place in society, and those with autism for instance are often said to be somehow trapped in 'a fortress' or behind 'a wall'. Even Jean Vanier (1998), whilst passionately advocating for equality and belonging for people with disability, still talks at times of disability as 'brokenness' (p. 23). Our perceptions of people with disabilities are often influenced then by unconscious hangovers from less-enlightened times, though Nussbaum (2007) reassures us that we are not in essence or by nature an unjust society and, even in Western societies dominated by economic motives and considerations of efficiency, *'the decency of human beings does aim at justice for its own sake'* (p. 160). So how just are we towards people with SLD and PMLD once they have left the protective confines of education? Do they enjoy the same social freedoms and outcomes as the rest of us?

In many, but not all, aspects of health, people with intellectual disabilities are disadvantaged when compared with their peers and, in some areas (e.g. mortality, mental health, speech and communication disorders) these differences are stark (Emerson and Hatton, 2013). Glover and Ayub (2010) found that people with all learning difficulties die on average 15 years earlier than the rest of the population and, if they have a co-occurring condition, on average 24 years earlier. Perry et al. (2011) explain this discrepancy at least in part by the fact that

> currently in the UK medical schools devote little time to training students about the specific health-care needs of people with learning disabilities, usually no more than one or two days over a 5 year course.
>
> (p. 12)

People with learning difficulties are more likely to experience living circumstances and life events associated with an increased risk of mental and physical health problems (Goward and Gething, 2005; O'Brien, 2016), with precipitating factors including poor social support, fewer friends, a lack of intimacy and social integration, isolation, and exclusion (BOND, 2013). Rates of mental illness are considerably higher for those with learning difficulties than in the general population. Holt et al. (2007) give a prevalence of mental illness for all people with learning difficulties as between 10% and 50%, whilst Goward and Gething (2005) put the range at between 10% and 80%. A figure of 40% is given more recently by both BOND (2013) and England's Department for Health (2011) and is comparable to statistics from some other countries, with Australia at 40% and South Africa at 31% (www.complexneeds.org.uk).

It is difficult to isolate statistics for people with SLD and PMLD, but Bradley et al. (2004) found a significant increase in symptoms of mental illness using the DASH II criteria (Diagnostic Assessment for the Severely Handicapped) in young people with autism and severe intellectual disability compared to those with autism alone. In the United Kingdom's Special Educational Needs and Disability Code of Practice (DfE, 2015), although the phrase 'mental health' appears 34 times, none of these instances are in the context of young people with complex needs and in fact there is an underlying implication in the document that mental health is considered separate to learning difficulties with the phrase '*learning difficulties or mental health issues*' (or is underscored) occurring twice in separate sections (6.21 and 6.22).

There is considerable evidence to indicate that people who have wider and closer social networks and people who report feeling connected to their local community tend to have better health (Stansfeld, 2006; Uchino, 2006; Murayama et al., 2012). Similar associations have been reported for people with intellectual disabilities, particularly in relation to the extent of contact with friends with intellectual disabilities (Emerson and Hatton, 2008; Shattuck et al., 2011). However, Emerson et al. (2005), reporting on results from the 2003/4 national survey of the life experiences of adults with intellectual disabilities in England, indicate that 58% of adults with intellectual disabilities had infrequent contact with their families (compared with just 9% of adults without intellectual disabilities) and 31% of adults with intellectual disabilities had no contact with friends (compared with just 3% of adults without intellectual disabilities). The most commonly reported barriers to having more social contact were:

- living too far away or problems with travelling (44%);
- not enough time (21%);
- lack of money (13%);
- not always enough support (11%);
- cannot get out or too ill (4%);
- afraid of going out (4%).

So, despite legislation such as the Special Educational Needs and Disability Act (2001), the Children and Families Act (2014), and the resulting SEND Code of Practice (2015), perhaps the United Kingdom is still not quite as just towards people with higher levels of need as we would like to think, and there is a significant disparity between theoretical models of justice and the reality in society as a whole. Further, there are no studies to suggest that, despite numerous and significant 'disability' legislation in the United States, Australia, and Italy over the last 30 years, the position of those with severe and profound learning difficulties is particularly more encouraging in these countries. As Johnson and Walmsley (2010) put it: '*the rhetoric of users being in the driving seat was subscribed to in theory, but did not match the reality*' (p. 158).

Nussbaum (2007) suggests that a reason for this may be that social justice is '*usually extrapolated from dominant discourse down to people with disabilities*' (p. 34) with the primary subjects of social justice being the same people who choose the principles, so largely not those with learning difficulties. Social theories to date, she points out, have been based on a general image of society as a '*contract for mutual advantage*' (p. 4) in which each of the parties is a productive individual, with Father Timothy Novis, in his foreword to Jarlath O'Brien's book, '*Don't Send Him in Tomorrow*' (2016), suggesting that investment in the younger generation in particular is looked on as a kind of mutually advantageous '*economic transaction*' (p. 4). So it is perhaps not surprising, Nussbaum (2007) maintains, that social contract theories to date have not really sought to include people with severe physical or mental impairments because they tend to be seen as non-contributors to a society built around production for profit, and this has been compounded by the fact that our value judgements about their lives and achievements are largely based on our own experiences and values, and not theirs. Bhogal (2014) posits that contractarians require a person to be rational in order to deserve certain goods, and therefore dignity, whilst also pointing out that the Capabilities Approach requires only that a person is social. Johnson and Walmsley (2010) also see this in terms of '*social role valorisation*' (Wolfensberger, 1983), in as much as despite years of debate around inclusion and integration, the social role of people with learning difficulties is simply not as valued as that of others and their 'success' – social or otherwise – is largely defined for them according to criteria which are often not applicable to their actual lived experience. When 'success' is achieved, it can often depend on the fact that their parents are educated, well off, and articulate, and surely, Nussbaum (2007) asks, a just society would not permit such crucial matters to depend on this kind of chance. The social inclusion and acceptance of citizens with mental or physical impairments then '*raises questions which go to the heart of the classical contractarian accounts of justice and social cooperation*' (p. 18), and these are issues, Nussbaum insists, which must be discussed and weighed by the whole of society in the same way that the whole of society takes responsibility for its views on race and gender.

This would be a significant task for any society to achieve, and would arguably take almost as long as it has taken society to take its faltering and often imperfect steps towards racial and sexual equality and acceptance, but that doesn't mean we shouldn't at least try to start correcting these manifest inequalities for people with SLD and PMLD. Public policy as we have seen, despite its best efforts, has still not managed adequately to address the place within society of this sizeable group of people, so clearly we may need to look beyond policy at our own values and perceptions so that the '*language of human flourishing*' (Nussbaum, 2007; 190) can be extended to these groups. Until the way we perceive and conceptualise people with SLD and PMLD is based more on where they actually are and not where we expect them to be (Lacey and Scull, 2015), we may well be unable to provide a more appropriate education for them as well. Johnson and Walmsley (2010) put it like this:

> For some people with high support needs or with little or no spoken language, the values underpinning the Western concept of a good life may need to be revisited.
>
> (p. 53)

And Ekins (2015) takes the same need for a paradigm shift into the education debate, stating:

> education needs to reflect a values-based approach to working towards an equitable inclusive society for all.
>
> (p. 172)

In the previous chapter, we discussed the fact that one of the reasons why people with the most severe and complex levels of learning difficulty have been denied a full role in society is because it has been felt their capacity for logic and reason is diminished (Nussbaum, 2007), as is their ability to make choices and communicate or behave in ways we can 'understand'. These are the very perceptions which we need to challenge if we are to redefine how we view these groups. Nussbaum reminds us that '*we all, more or less have the same sort of reason*' (p. 159), and our own reason is not inherently any more or less reliable than that of someone with severe or profound learning difficulties. It is simply framed differently. History, ancient and modern, is littered with examples of reason appearing to have been abandoned even by those we think are most wise, and choices are made which are constantly not in our own or anyone's best interests, so what right have we to decide that people whose capacity for 'reason' and 'choice' we judge to be impaired have less right to a good life than the rest of us?

Johnson and Walmsley (2010) agree that we respond to people with SLD and PMLD in ways which imply that they have a '*flawed reasoning*' (p. 117), and that this process starts in school. School staff are '*cast as a way to compensate for a perceived lack of reason*' (p. 151) in the same way that '*technology makes up for the space created by the impairment*' (p. 161). In practice, this means that we have to be assiduous in ensuring that when working with children, young people, and adults who are open to being interpreted into disability, engagements with key decision-making involves people who (i) are skilled and experienced in working with those with SLD and PMLD and (ii) know the individual really well. In recognition of this, Crombie et al.'s (2014) action research at Pear Tree (Special) School in Lancashire, England, a serially Ofsted-rated outstanding school, makes a powerful argument for the necessity of high-quality professional competence:

> Our task has been to identify those implicit, unnoticed, unconscious professional practices in order then to find ways to rebalance staff training and support to enable their expression for the benefit of children and young people. From the outset there has been a concern for 'pupil voice' (however that is expressed) and recognition of the centrality of adult–child relationships to effective professional practice.
>
> (Crombie et al., 2014, 9)

When concern for establishing agency is not high on the agenda or overridden by considerations of functional necessity and sensible risk awareness, there can be failures to register any significant '*appreciation of difference*' (Johnson and Walmsley, 2010, 163) and take account of the person's '*subjective being*' (p. 126). The second author saw an example of this a few years ago when he was working in a special school as a teacher of young people aged 14–19 with SLD and PMLD. It was the afternoon and the pupils had been in the small stuffy classroom all day. One or two of them were beginning to get a bit irritable, as indeed anyone would who had been confined anywhere for a similar length of time. 'Maeve' was a wheelchair user with cerebral palsy who had little recognizable spoken language, though did express herself very clearly and eloquently in sounds. She came from a home full of space and light and love and her parents were absolutely committed to supporting her to live a full and active life in ways which suited her. The teacher's concern on that day was that Maeve had spent far longer contained in one room than her parents would ever allowed to have happened at home, and she was beginning to express this through sound and gesture. A relatively new teaching assistant was asked to take Maeve out around the school grounds and maybe even along a quiet lane which adjoined the school. So quite correctly the TA put Maeve in her coat and went out. Five minutes later, they returned, the TA took Maeve's coat off, and brought her back in the classroom. 'What's going on?' asked the teacher. 'Why are you back so soon?' 'It looked like it was going to rain', answered the TA.

Now arguably, the teacher had made assumptions himself about Maeve's reasoned choices and inner life, but those assumptions were at least based on three important things which put Maeve at the centre of his decision-making, as well as the knowledge that, as Nussbaum herself noted, citizens with impairment often have diminished opportunities to enjoy nature.

- He had been Maeve's teacher for three years, and so felt he knew her well enough to know when she was expressing frustration at a situation and a need for a change.
- His experience with Maeve had taught him that she loved the sights, sounds, and smells of the countryside.
- Maeve's parents – who knew her far better than any of the staff ever would – understood instinctively that a classroom was not often the best place for Maeve to flourish, and time spent outside was often more valuable to Maeve's development and learning, even if it looked like it was going to rain.

The TA, however – well meaning, but inexperienced and new to the class – had almost certainly based her own decision to return from the walk so soon entirely on her own reasoning and values, and not in any way on Maeve's. Of course, it takes a wise and skilled teaching assistant, advocate, or key worker to take the time really to get to know the person and then effectively step back, be patient, and accept that the possible rational responses to any given situation available to the person in their care are not necessarily the same as his or her own, but just as valid and worth exploring if not actually enacting. What is required urgently then, according to Johnson and Walmsley (2010), is education for all people working with those with learning difficulties that '*places the good life and how to achieve it at the centre of their work*' (p. 175).

It never did rain that day.

Reasoning then, as displayed by someone with SLD or PMLD, can be just as valid as our own and very few, if any, of these young people, even in the most extreme circumstances, do something which doesn't have a valid internal logic behind it and which in fact reflects the same kind of internal logic anyone might display in a similar situation. When really distressed, 'Kevin', a 16-year-old non-verbal autistic boy with additional severe learning difficulties, could

> bang his head as hard as he can on the walls, bite his hands and punch himself. He also bites other people. Not harmless little nips, but proper bites which draw blood.
>
> (Colley, 2013, 15)

One day he bit his teacher so hard on the forearm that the teacher needed medical treatment. On the surface biting another person seems like an irrational and animalistic act and as such it tends to elicit disgust and censure as we project our own fear of animalistic immorality onto the less powerful (Nussbaum, 2004). A close examination of the circumstances however reveals that this young man was acting entirely logically and reasonably in the terms available to him. Kevin was being restrained by two teaching assistants and, even though they were using recognised and appropriate holds which they had been trained to carry out, restraint is still invasive. When it appeared he had calmed down, the teacher took over and told the people holding Kevin to let him go gently. As soon as he was free Kevin got up very quickly but still in quite an agitated state. He paced up and down and came very close to the teacher, who flinched. Sensing perhaps an increased tension, Kevin bit the teacher on the arm. He then gradually calmed down, began crying, and the teacher made him a cup of tea. Now, if a young man with no learning difficulties at all was being restrained and didn't fully understand why, as soon as he was released he would certainly be pretty angry, and may even shout, and other people would probably appreciate that shouting angrily was a reasonable emotional response to the situation. He may not bite someone, but in Kevin's case, he didn't have a voice – either literally or metaphorically – and like some other people with SLD or PMLD, biting was something he did when distressed. So when the teacher flinched, he probably saw that as another potential threat and responded in actually the only way he could 'reasonably' respond at that time and in that place.

O'Brien (2016) is rightly concerned that 'behaviour' and 'special educational needs' are seen as interchangeable by some practitioners and that most strategies to address challenging behaviour are based on the unspoken rule: *'Let's make them more like us'* (p. 30). Nussbaum (2004) sees this in terms of our understanding of 'normality', which tends to be twofold: the mathematical statistical norm and the concept of good and bad. She questions why this should be so when so many things that are not normal or usual are good, and vice versa. Her answer is that approaching anything outside of normal as bad allows us to feel protected and distanced from the imperfections about which we feel the deepest shame and horror, such as extremes of deformity, mental incapacity, or behaviour. But in fact of course 'they' are like us and not like us at the same time and asserting this in school and in the public domain is key to re-imagining how society might look if people with SLD and PMLD are to be truly valued and included in it. Clearly, many people do this already, though this sometimes comes with conditions attached: the father who tries to stop his autistic son 'hand flapping' in supermarkets though doesn't mind him doing it at home; the passer-by who – like some Victorian philanthropist – offers a pound to the teacher when she sees a class of young people with SLD and PMLD in the street (this has happened to both authors more than once), and this incident described in Solomon (2014) by the mother of a young girl with autism who takes off her pad in a public swimming pool:

> One of the mothers screamed 'Contamination! Contamination! Then all of the others began to yank their children out of the water. Lifeguards blew whistles and screamed, and Cece stood amid the chaos, laughing uproariously.
>
> (p. 226)

Maybe acceptance, inclusion, and belonging for the most vulnerable is still just out of reach. Robert Orr, in a recent post on the SLD Forum, puts it like this: *'There must be room in this world for people who are great spitters and biters; the knack is to find that space'* (Orr, 2016).

Behaviour, of course, is communication (Imray, 2008; Imray and Hewett, 2015) and being disabled certainly does not mean you have nothing to say or have no opinions. The opinions of people with SLD and PMLD can be just as nuanced and diverse as the rest of us, and in view of their life experience and the often unthinking treatment we mete out to them, pretty forceful too. The communication of a person with severe or profound and multiple needs is flexible and multi-modal, and very often and especially when there is attendant autism, the propensity for language and for communication go off in separate directions (Jordan, 2001). As practitioners however we still all too often seem to forget this and the most common alternative communication systems used with non-verbal people with SLD and PMLD are symbolic or representational and are more or less based on the assumption that what is lacking and therefore needs to be replaced by a symbol or picture are simply words. Language however is a complex cognitive process that develops over time in a social context (Sharma and Cockerill, 2014; Equals, 2016b). Where this social context and the vital cultural transmissions (Jordan, 2001) which accompany it have followed atypical lines for a person with severe learning difficulties, the potential for either real or symbolic language development and acquisition is significantly restricted. Ouvry (1987) agrees that it can sometimes be assumed that once an alternative symbol-based communication system is introduced, children with SLD or PMLD will have the means to communicate, without considering that their life experience up to that point and the very different social and cognitive skills they have gained probably means that what they are wanting to communicate and how they want to communicate it might be very different from our expectations. As Vanier (1998) reminds us: '*we are not skilled at listening to the wisdom of those whose life patterns are outside the social norm*' (p. 46), and it is up to us – the researchers, teachers, and other practitioners – to find creative ways of listening.

Colley (2013) describes spending time with a young man named 'Karl' at the beginning of the year in his new class. Karl was non-verbal and had a reputation for being 'difficult', especially in situations which were new and unfamiliar to him. Colley and a colleague had two options: they could show Karl a number of pre-prepared laminated pictures representing activities he might be interested in, and this would certainly appear to be giving Karl some kind of 'choice'. Alternatively they could hand over the communication process to Karl. This would take time and patience on the teachers' part, but then people with severe learning difficulties are also usually expected to share our own concepts of time, so perhaps in this instance they could hand that over too.

The teachers made as many class areas and resources accessible to Karl as possible. They told him he could do whatever he wanted and go wherever he wanted and then they sat down and waited. At first, and possibly not surprisingly as this was a very different approach to the one he was used to, Karl became anxious. He hit himself a few times and pushed his head against the teachers', who tried very hard not to react. Over the next hour, Karl slowly calmed – through diminishing peaks and troughs – and his difficult behaviours reduced. He moved around the classrooms, opening things, tipping some things out, smelling things, licking things. Eventually, he took a crayon and piece of paper from a cupboard, sat down, and began to draw. During that hour, Karl had expressed plenty of completely valid opinions. He had expressed anxiety at being in an unfamiliar place with unfamiliar people, he had explored and rejected several resources and activities, and finally he had 'told' his teachers that what he wanted to do was to draw.

Of course it was not only Karl's right to express opinions and make choices that was important, it was also his autonomy, his right to '*control his material environment*' (Johnson and Walmsley, 2010, p. 194), and the rights of all people with SLD and PMLD to be an '*active agent in their own lives*' (p. 125). To feel and be independent. The values which underpin our perceptions of independence are central to a revalorisation of what a good life, and a good education, might look like for this group and we cannot hope in this book to discuss social justice without addressing the dilemmas around care and autonomy in the wider social context and unpicking a little what dependence and independence mean or could mean.

Taylor (2014) writes: '*Today, the independence imperative is stronger than ever*' (p. 248). When we talk about 'the good life', what we usually mean is an independent life where someone has the means to choose what to do, when to do it, and who to do it with. To need other people on a day-to-day basis, Taylor argues, is seen as '*a mark of emotional debility*' (p. 248) and, as such, those who need other people the most are trapped at the very far end of Nussbaum's '*single linear ranking of relative social positions*' (p. 141). However, the concept of adult autonomy, Taylor notes, is '*a fantasy*' (p. 260). True independence is rooted in social connection and without this, '*it is mere isolation and loneliness*' (p. 252). In reality '*people depend on other people to lead a liveable life*' (p. 264) and the quality and shape of social networks are central to the well-being of us all, and certainly no less for those with the highest level of need. Yet the social connections of people with SLD and PMLD are very largely ignored, for as Abbot and McConkey (2006) note,

> of all the assessments done on people with learning difficulties, the one least likely to be carried out is an examination of their friendships.
>
> (p. 469)

And these friendships will include people who are paid to spend time with those with disabilities. Indeed, sometimes these can be the very best of friendships. If we are truly to value people with the highest level of need, and accord them equality and a good life, we need also to redefine our '*notions of guardianship*' (Nussbaum, 2010, 76) and to value and celebrate the relationships of dependency which they count on in their day-to-day lives, which in most cases of course involves their parents or carers. Here again, though, there is very little justice, or as O'Brien (2016) so brilliantly puts it:

> There is a world of difference between working with children and learning difficulties and being the parent of a child with learning difficulties. One comes with a salary, pension and several weeks off per year. The other does not.
>
> (p. 83)

To be the parent or carer of someone with SLD or PMLD can often be a very difficult life indeed. Nussbaum (2007) calls this the *'secondary handicap'* (p. 142) and being a carer is all too often isolating, frustrating, and economically challenging. Policy of course can and should correct this injustice by repositioning *'care as a primary social entitlement'* (p. 178). Socially, the cared for and the care giver are often on an equal footing, but *'dignity can also be found of relations of dependency'* (p. 218) and as a society we need to ask ourselves if we value reciprocity as much as we do independence, because only then can we hope to create what Nussbaum calls *'a full and equal citizenship of people with physical impairments, and of those who care for them'* (p. 99).

Paid work is of course very often seen as a key driver of attaining independence and a good life, and there seems no good reason why people with moderate and severe learning difficulties should not work. UK studies indicate however that only 5.8% of working-age adults with intellectual disabilities are in any form of paid employment (Mencap, 2016), with just 2% of men and less than 1% of women working for 30 or more hours per week (Emerson et al., 2012; ONS, 2015), as well as usually earning less (O'Brien, 2016). The number of jobs which do not require literacy and numeracy have undoubtedly diminished in countries such as the United Kingdom over the last 50 years, which may well account for the fact that in a recent Mencap survey, 62% of the public said they have never worked with someone who has a learning disability (Mencap, 2016). We are somewhat surprised that 38% of the public have since this does not tie in with our knowledge of the work prospects of school leavers with learning difficulties, despite the remarkable amount of effort in planning and organising work experience for the 16-plus age group that goes on in the vast majority of UK special schools. It seems to us that this is an issue in urgent need of more action research.

Mencap (2016) suggest that amongst other things, governments need to improve access to apprenticeships, grow the number of supported internships, increase support for employers wanting to take on staff with a learning disability, and boost the number of job coaches. To this we would add the necessity of directly educating the public through a nationwide advertising campaign that highlights the ethical and moral responsibility that society holds for all its citizens. This voluntary approach may however not be enough. It is reasonable to assume that the term 'learning difficulties' is a construct of the industrial revolution (Hurley, 1969; Pick, 1989) and it may therefore be reasonable to expect the beneficiaries of the industrial revolution to have a far greater obligation towards all citizens within a capitalist economy. This may include legislation to instruct companies of a certain size to employ, say, 1% of their workforce from those with disabilities.

It is, however, highly likely that the issue of 'labelling' and the deleterious effects of labelling is a real consideration in the world of work. We remain vociferous defenders of the necessity of an accurate indication of levels of learning difficulty in education, so that a fit-for-purpose pedagogy and curriculum can be ascribed, but we recognise that general social understandings and tolerance of those with SLD and PMLD may well be lacking, especially in their potential and abilities in the world of work. The social advantages of having a job, as well as a sense of purpose, heightened self-esteem, and a sense of belonging and contribution, are clear. Not working automatically throws people back on the benefits system, ensuring that they are less able to access that good life or attain a level of financial comfort and autonomy available to those who do work. In the United Kingdom at least, we seem to have accepted the 'inability' of those with SLD and PMLD to work, yet this should be intolerable to any civilised society. We believe that the enormous good will within the academic community towards those with disabilities could be more usefully garnered to fighting for real social inclusion, rather than almost exclusively fighting for educational inclusion.

Work can provide an essential sense of belonging and Vanier (1998) situates belonging as '*the fulcrum point for the individual between a sense of self and a sense of society*' (p. 57). Johnson and Walmsley (2010) have even proposed that 'belonging' might replace the term 'inclusion' in future policy and practice. A good life for people with SLD or PMLD, they propose, should be based on '*belonging and relationship building*' (p. 131). Nussbaum too is clear on this. We must draw back from the '*ranking of lives*' (2011b, 36) and acknowledge that there is in fact a very real '*continuity between so-called normal people and people with impairments*' (2007, 190). A continuity, not a ranking, in which we acknowledge our shared and linked humanity. Our mutual belonging. This would be the foundation of a good life for all, a life where we learn from each other rather than from the top down, a life with space for '*diverse possibilities*' (p 182) to flourish and where equality means more than just access to buildings and transport but living in '*multifarious communities*' (p 70), and above all one in which we '*protect pluralism*' (p 79) and truly value humanity in all its diversity. We do not seek to describe what these communities might look like, but we do propose that a radical reshaping of education for these young people may begin, slowly, to point towards a good life which '*emerges from within the person*' (Johnson and Walmsley, 2010, 173). To do this, as we have seen, will mean challenging many of our entrenched values and perceptions, and will entail redefining what we mean by 'outcomes' for our learners with the highest level of need (Boddison, 2016). Reframing specific SLD and PMLD pedagogies and curricula will underpin this paradigm shift and, far from excluding young people with SLD and PMLD from the education system, will truly prepare them, and us, for a life of inclusion, purpose, and belonging.

9   Conclusion
And a way forward?

At the very beginning of this book, we stated that the truth of educational inclusion is neither eternal nor unarguable. However laudable the ideals, it doesn't work and it never has worked. Inclusion is dead.

In the United Kingdom at least, we may not even have noticed this were it not for those 50,000 or so young people on the SLD and PMLD spectrums. They told us something was wrong. They pointed out that the ideal of inclusion wasn't quite what it seemed. Despite the rhetoric, despite the spin, it has been dying on its feet, and it has died because its potential lifeblood – the most vulnerable and dispossessed – are not part of it at all, and because they aren't part of it, any concept of inclusion for all becomes a nonsense. All must mean all, and if it doesn't, the underlying case for inclusion, however much we moderate the definition, becomes too weak to sustain.

We are not, of course, the first to suggest this. In the same year as the Salamanca Statement, Fuchs and Fuchs were pleading the case for special education. It is 'special' they said, for a reason, because '*it is unique in ways that general education is not and probably never can be*' (Fuchs and Fuchs, 1994, 20).

In 2005, full inclusion was described as

> contrary to common sense, inconsistent with what we know about disabilities, and devoid of credible supporting evidence.
>
> (Mock and Kauffman, 2005, 113)

We believe both of these statements to be true, finding no logic for the notion that a common school and/or a common class and/or a common curriculum can improve *educational* outcomes for those on the SLD and PMLD spectrums. Parents and carers of children with SLD or PMLD may well choose an inclusive setting for their child, and if the setting is exceptional, the learner may thrive educationally, but this will be despite the setting and the curriculum and not because of them.

But what of social inclusion? The emphasis given to the role of education in being the main provider of social inclusion almost acts as an apology for the restricted educational opportunities offered. It is as though inclusionists are saying, '*Well, they might fail educationally but at least they'll have a wonderful social life.*' But this is not proven either. There are no definitive studies which might lead us to believe that friendships made in school with children on the SLD and PMLD spectrums are anything other than transient, if indeed they happen at all (Wendelborg and Kvello, 2010; Locke et al., 2010; Carman and Chapparo, 2012). In fact we would venture as far as to say that the fact that social inclusion is not Social Inclusion, a subject with capital letters to be studied and learned and given time on the curriculum, gives most schools ample opportunity to pay lip service to the concept. We do not blame schools or school leaders or teachers for this – they have directives from above which directly compromise their ability to make certain choices that involve time away from academic subject-based teaching and learning. We do not, however, have to have all children in the same class or even in the same school to make social inclusion a valuable, worthwhile, achievable, and realistic goal. We cannot expect schools to take social inclusion seriously if we as a society don't take it seriously, if we as a society don't allocate time and a statutory insistence that it takes place. Schools have, in the United Kingdom at least, become places where children go to succeed in exams, the pinnacle being the school leaving exams (GCSE's – General Certificate of Secondary Education), generally taken at the age of 16. Schools' successes are measured against every child achieving at least five of these at grades above a 'C', including English and maths, or in preparing children for such an achievement. That 65% of pupils in England and Wales hit this mark in 2015 may be regarded as cause for celebration; though of course 35% did not. And the United Kingdom's solution to this dilemma? Keep them at school for even longer so that they have even longer to fail in the system.

We as a society in the United Kingdom seem to have fallen under the inclusionist spell that equity demands that every single person must have the same; that it is iniquitous to offer a different curriculum, because that means giving up on children, judging them as failures, labelling them as different. Perhaps, however, the lessons to be learned from those on the SLD and PMLD spectrums regarding different pedagogy and curricula need to be looked at more closely for other groups as well. We refer again to Carpenter's insistence on the rising of a 'new generation' of children with complex needs who are 'pedagogically bereft' (Carpenter, 2011; Carpenter et al., 2016) and there are of course the very many pupils, especially those with social, emotional, and behavioural difficulties, who are totally disengaged with the education system. Like the seven learners at St Ann's School described in Chapter 7, like Kevin and Maeve and Karl described in Chapter 8, perhaps we need to offer reasons for the many disengaged to want to join in. Student voice must be listened to if education is not just going to be about educating those who are willing to comply. This means listening to behaviours and acting upon what these behaviours are telling us, not merely insisting that everyone does the same. We must give children and young people a reason to belong, and whilst it may be ideal that this happens in the same classroom, in the same school, and studying the same curriculum, the evidence tells us that this is not possible, however much we might like it to be so.

So we have gone back to basics and asked a fundamental question: why are we teaching what we are teaching? We found that however wonderful the education system in the United Kingdom is, and in very many ways it is wonderful, it is geared like the majority of Western, First World education systems to the perceived needs of the norm to achieve 'minimum' academic standards within curriculums largely unchallenged for nearly a century, pass exams, and prepare for life at work. The continuing quest to include 'all' in this essentially economic, academic, and memory-based project has spewed out a whole raft of unintended consequences which exacerbate the unpreparedness of school leavers with SLD and PMLD for the life they will lead after school, into middle age, and beyond. When the goals of education have nothing to do with what is meaningful to particular groups of people, we merely compound their failure and the failure of society itself.

We therefore argue for a change, for education to become something of real and intrinsic value to every person, including those with SLD and PMLD, and to do that we need to think differently. Education needs to be seen as a means of fostering all learners' opportunities to maximise their potential to do the very best they can do and to be the very best they can be, irrespective of their individual circumstances. Not in our terms, not in terms of an economic project, but in their own terms. To do this, we need to listen. Not to the ideologues, not to the cynics, but to the young people themselves. They each have a voice, an opinion, and we need to find ways to listen. And then we need to go further. We need to find a commonality between education and post education, because to be truly valid, an education for a young person with SLD or PMLD must reach beyond school. In fact it must in itself be about the whole of a person's life, the whole of their being. And if we can achieve that for all these young people with SLD or PMLD, how many other people in education might this new paradigm fit?

We have suggested that inclusion is dead, but we hope also that this book has pointed towards a new beginning: we want inclusion to redefine itself as a living, breathing thing with real value and real purpose. Not just educational inclusion, but real and meaningful social inclusion, not only for those with SLD and PMLD, but maybe also for many, many more for whom the current education system is no longer fit for purpose. Long live inclusion!

References

Abbott, S. and McConkey, R. (2006) The barriers to social inclusion as perceived by people with intellectual disabilities. *Journal of Intellectual Disabilities* 10 (3): 275–287.

Adams, S. (2001) *When Did Ignorance Become a Point of View?* Kansas City: Boxtree.

Ainscow, M. (2005) Developing inclusive education systems: What are the levers for change? *Journal of Educational Change* 6 (2): 109–124.

Ainscow, M. (2006) Towards a more inclusive education system: Where next for special schools? in R. Cigman (ed) *Included of Excluded? The Challenge of the Mainstream for Some SEN Children.* London: Routledge.

Ainscow, M. (2016) *Struggles for Equity in Education.* Abingdon: Routledge.

Ainscow, M., Dyson, A., Goldrick, S. and West, M. (2012) *Developing Equitable Education Systems.* Abingdon: Routledge.

Aird, R. (2001) *The Education and Care of Children With Profound and Multiple Learning Difficulties.* London: David Fulton.

Aitken, S. and Buultjens, M. (1992) *Vision for Doing: Assessing Functional Vision of Learners Who Are Multiply Disabled.* Edinburgh: Moray House.

Alexander, R. (2004) Still no pedagogy? Principle, pragmatism and compliance in primary education. *Cambridge Journal of Education* 34 (1): 7–33.

Allan, J. (2013) Inclusion: Patterns and possibilities. *Zeitschrift für Inklusion* 4. Available at http://inklusion-online.net/index.php/inklusion-online/article/view/31/31 Accessed 22nd June 2016.

Alloway, T. P. and Alloway, R. G. (2015) *Understanding Working Memory* (2nd ed.). London: Sage.

Alloway, T. P., Gathercole, S. E., Kirkwood, H. J. and Elliot, J. E. (2009) The cognitive and behavioural characteristics of children with low working memory. *Child Development* 80: 606–621.

Anderson, J. and Boyle, C. (2015) Inclusive education in Australia: Rhetoric, reality and the road ahead. *Support for Learning* 30 (1): 4–22.

ASCET. (1984) *Advice: Teacher Training and Special Educational Needs.* London: Advisory Committee on the Supply and Education of Teachers.

Attwood, L. (2013) The real implications of 'benevolent' SEN reform. *Support for Learning* 28 (4): 181–187.

Avramides, E. and Norwich, B. (2002) Teachers' attitudes towards integration/inclusion: A review of the literature. *European Journal of Special Needs Education* 17 (2): 129–147.

Ayres, K. M., Lowery, K. A., Douglas, K. H. and Sievers, C. (2011) I can identify Saturn but I can't brush my teeth: What happens when the curricular focus for students with severe disabilities shifts. *Education and Training in Autism and Developmental Disabilities* 46: 11–21.

Ayres, K. M., Lowery, K. A., Douglas, K. H. and Sievers, C. (2012) The question still remains: What happens when the curricular focus for students with severe disabilities shifts? A reply to Courtade, Spooner, Browder, and Jimenez (2012). *Education and Training in Autism and Developmental Disabilities* 47 (1): 14–22.

Bhogal, K. (2014) Justice and the Exclusion of Disabled People. Unpublished Masters Dissertation. University of Birmingham.

Blower, C. (2015) Inclusive thinking. *The Teacher Magazine*. London: National Union of Teachers.

Boddison, A. (2016) The outlook for children and young adults with SEND – remaining challenges and next steps forward in *Westminster Education Forum Keynote Seminar: Policy Priorities for SEND*, London, 3rd November 2016.

BOND. (2013) *Children and Young People With Learning Disabilities – Understanding Their Mental Health*. Available at www.youngminds.org.uk/assets/0000/9593/Children_and_Young_People_with_Learning_Disabilities_intro.pdf.

Booth, T., Ainscow, M., Black-Hawkins, K., Vaughan, M. and Shaw, L. (2000) *The Index for Inclusion: Developing Learning and Participation in Schools*. Bristol: CSIE.

Bovair, K., Carpenter, B. and Upton, G. (eds) (1992) *Special Curricula Needs*. London: David Fulton and NASEN.

Boyle, C. and Topping, K. (2012) *What Works in Inclusion?* Maidenhead: Open University Press.

Bradley, E. A., Summers, J. A., Wood, H. L. and Bryson, S. E. (2004) Comparing rates of psychiatric and behavior disorders in adolescents and young adults with severe intellectual disability with and without autism. *Journal of Autism and Developmental Disorders* 34 (2): 151–161.

Bratlinger, E. (1997) Using ideology: Cases of nonrecognition of the politics of research and practice in special education. *Review of Educational Research* 67: 425–459.

The Bridge School. (2010) *Curriculum for Pupils With Profound and Multiple Learning Difficulties*. London: The Bridge School. Available at www.thebridgelondon.co.uk/assets/filemanager/downloads/The%20Bridge%20London%20PMLD%20Curriculum.pdf.

Briggs, S. (2016) *Meeting Special Educational Needs in Primary Classrooms*. Abingdon: Routledge.

Broderick, A. A. and Ne'eman, A. (2008) Autism as metaphor: Narrative and Counter Narrative. *International Journal of Inclusive Education* 12 (5–6): 459–476.

Brown, E. (1996) *Religious Education for All*. London: David Fulton.

Brown, I., Hatton, C. and Emerson, E. (2013) Quality of life indicators for individuals with intellectual disabilities: Extending current practice. *Intellectual and Developmental Disabilities* 51 (5): 316–332.

Bruner, J. S. (2009) *The Process of Education*. Cambridge, MA: Harvard University Press.

Burgoyne, K., Duff, F. J., Clarke, P. J., Buckley, S., Snowling, M. J. and Hulme, C. (2012) Efficacy of a reading and language intervention for children with Down syndrome: A randomized controlled trial. *The Journal of Child Psychology and Psychiatry* 53 (10): 1044–1053.

Burgoyne, K., Duff, F. J., Snowling, M. J., Buckley, S. and Hulme, C. (2013) Training phoneme blending skills in children with Down syndrome. *Child Language Teaching and Therapy* 29: 273–290.

Byers, R. and Lawson, H. (2015) Priorities, products and process: Developments in providing a curriculum for learners with SLD/PMLD in P. Lacey, R. Ashdown, P. Jones, H. Lawson and M. Pipe (eds) *The Routledge Companion to Severe Profound and Multiple Learning Difficulties*. London: Routledge.

Cameron, D. L. (2014) An examination of teacher – student interactions in inclusive classrooms: Teacher interviews and classroom observations. *Journal of Research in Special Educational Needs* 14 (4): 264–273.

Carman, S. N. and Chapparo, C. J. (2012) Children who experience difficulties with learning: Mother and child perceptions of social competence. *Australian Occupational Therapy Journal* 59 (5): 339–346.

Carpenter, B. (2011) Pedagogically Bereft!: Improving learning outcomes for children with foetal alcohol spectrum disorders. *British Journal of Special Education* 38 (1): 38–43.

Carpenter, B., Carpenter, J., Egerton, J. and Cockbill, B. (2016) The engagement for learning framework: Connecting with learning and evidencing progress for children with autism spectrum conditions. *Advances in Autism* 2 (1): 12–23.

Carpenter, B., Egerton, J., Cockbill, B., Bloom, T., Fotheringham, J., Rawson, H. and Thistlethwaite, J. (2015) *Engaging Learners With Complex Learning Difficulties and Disabilities*. Abingdon: Routledge.

Carter, A. (2015) Carter review of initial teacher training Dept. for Education Castle Wood School (2012) The Castle Wood Informal (P1–P4) Curriculum. Coventry. Castle Wood School. Available at www.castlewood.coventry.sch.uk.

Chapman, R. S. (2003) Language and communication in individuals with Down syndrome in L. Abbeduto (ed) *International Review of Research in Mental Retardation: Language and Communication*. Vol. 27. San Diego, CA: Academic Press, 1–34.

Cigman, R. (2007) *Included or Excluded? The Challenge of the Mainstream for Some Special Educational Needs Children*. London: Routledge.

Clough, P. and Nutbrown. C. (2002) A Students Guide to Methodology. London: Sage Publications.

Clough, P. and Nutbrown, C. (2005) Inclusion and development in the early years: Making inclusion conventional? *Child Care in Practice* 11 (2): 99–102.

Colley, A. (2013) *Personalised Learning for Young People With Profound and Multiple Learning Difficulties*. London: Jessica Kingsley.

Conway, R. (2012) Inclusive schools in Australia: Rhetoric and practice in C. Boyle and K. Topping (eds) *What Works in Inclusion?* Maidenhead: Open University Press.

Corbett, J. and Norwich, B. (2005) Common or specialised pedagogy? in M. Nind, J. Rix, K. Sheehy and K. Simmons (eds) *Curriculum and Pedagogy in Inclusive Education: Values and Practice.* Abingdon: RoutledgeFalmer.

Coupe O'Kane, J. and Goldbart, J. (1998) *Communication Before Speech.* London: David Fulton.

Courtade, G., Spooner, F., Browder, D. and Jimenez, B. (2012) Seven reasons to promote standards-based instruction for students with severe disabilities: A reply to Ayres, Lowery, Douglas, & Sievers (2011). *Education and Training in Autism and Developmental Disabilities* 47: 3–13.

Cowan, N. and Alloway, T. P. (2008) The development of working memory in childhood in M. Courgae and N. Cowans (eds) *Development of Memory in Infancy and Childhood* (2nd ed.). Hove: Psychology Press, 303–342.

Crombie, R., Sullivan, L., Walker, K. and Warnock, R. (2014) Unconscious and unnoticed professional practice within an outstanding school for children and young people with complex learning difficulties and disabilities. *Support for Learning* 29 (1): 7–23.

CSIE. (2008) *Ten Reasons for Inclusion: Centre for Studies in Inclusive Education.* Available at www.csie.org.uk/resources/ten-reasons-02.pdf.

Davies, G. (2015) *Developing Memory Skills in the Primary Classroom.* Abingdon: Routledge.

Davis, P. and Florian, L. (2004) *Teaching Strategies and Approaches for Pupils With Special Educational Needs: A Scoping Study.* Nottingham: DfES Publications.

Department for Education. (2011) *Glossary of Special Educational Needs (SEN) Terminology.* Available at http://webarchive.nationalarchives.gov.uk/2013012312 4929/www.education.gov.uk/a0013104/glossary-of-special-educational-needs-sen-terminology Accessed 21st July 2016.

Department for Education. (2012) *Glossary of Special Educational Needs (SEN) Terminology.* Available at http://webarchive.nationalarchives.gov.uk/20130123124929/www.education.gov.uk/a0013104/glossary-of-special-educational-needs-sen-terminology Accessed 8th February 2016.

Department for Education. (2013) *The National Curriculum in England: Framework Document.* July 2014. Available at www.gov.uk/dfe/nationalcurriculum.

Department for Education. (2014a) *Performance – P Scale – Attainment Targets for Pupils With Special Educational Needs.* Available at www.gov.uk/ . . . /p-scales-attainment-targets-for-pupils-with-sen Accessed 18th February 2016.

Department for Education. (2014b) *Special Educational Needs and Disability Code of Practice: 0–25 Years.* London: Department for Education.

Department for Education. (2015) *The Special Educational Needs and Disability Code of Practice: 0 – 25 years.* London. Department of Health / Department of Education.

Department of Education and Science. (1981) *Education Act.* London: HMSO.

Department of Health. (2011) *No Health without Mental Health: a cross government mental health outcomes strategy for people of all ages* (2011). London. Her Majesty's Government / Department of Health.

Dunst, C. (1980) *A Clinical and Educational Manual for Use With the Uzgiris and Hunt Scales of Infant Psychological Development*. Austin, TX: Pro-Ed.

Ekins, A. (2015) *The Changing Face of Special Educational Needs*. London: Routledge.

Emerson, E. (2001) *Challenging Behaviour: Analysis and Intervention in People With Severe Intellectual Disabilities*. Cambridge: Cambridge University Press.

Emerson, E. and Hatton, C. (2008) The self-reported well-being of women and men with intellectual disabilities in England. *American Journal on Mental Retardation* 113: 143–155.

Emerson, E. and Hatton, C. (2013) *Health Inequalities and People With Intellectual Disabilities*. Cambridge: Cambridge University Press.

Emerson, E., Hatton, C., Robertson, J. et al. (2012) *People With Learning Disabilities in England: 2011*. Durham: Improving Health and Lives: Learning Disabilities Observatory.

Emerson, E., Malam, S., Davies, I. and Spencer, K. (2005) *Adults With Learning Difficulties in England 2003/4*. Leeds: Health and Social Care Information Centre.

Equals. (2016a) *The Equals Semi-Formal Curriculum for SLD and MLD*. Newcastle Equals. Available at www.equals.co.uk.

Equals. (2016b) *My Communication*. Newcastle Equals. Available at http://equals.co.uk/semi-formal-sow/.

Evans, J. and Lunt, I. (2002) Inclusive education: Are there limits? *European Journal of Special Needs Education* 17 (1): 1–14.

Fergusson, A., Howley, M., Rose, R. and Allen, R. (2015) Hidden behind a label: An uneasy relationship between mental health and special needs in P. Lacey, R. Ashdown, P. Jones, H. Lawson and M. Pipe (eds) *The Routledge Companion to Severe Profound and Multiple Learning Difficulties*. London: Routledge.

Florian, L. (1998) Inclusive practice: What, why and how? in C. Tilstone, L. Florian and R. Rose (eds) *Promoting Inclusive Practice*. London: Routledge.

Florian, L. (2009) Towards inclusive pedagogy in P. Hicks, R. Kershner and P. Farrell (eds) *Psychology for Inclusive Education: New Directions in Theory and Practice*. London: Routledge.

Florian, L. (2010a) The concept of inclusive pedagogy in F. Hallett and G. Hallett (eds) *Transforming the Role of the SENCO: Achieving the National Award for SEN Coordination*. Maidenhead: Open University Press.

Florian, L. (2010b) Special education in an era of inclusion: The end of special education or a new beginning? *The Psychology of Education Review* 34 (2): 22–29.

Florian, L. (2014) Reimagining special Education: Why new approaches are needed in L. Florian (ed) *The Sage Handbook of Special Education* (2nd ed.). London: Sage.

Florian, L. and Black-Hawkins, K. (2011) Exploring inclusive pedagogy. *British Educational Research Journal* 37 (5): 813–828.

Florian, L. and Hegarty, J. (2004) *ICT & Special Educational Needs: A Tool for Inclusion*. Buckinghamshire: Open University Press.

Forlin, C., Sharma, U. and Loreman, T. (2014) Predictors of improved teaching efficacy following basic training for inclusion in Hong Kong. *International Journal of Inclusive Education* 18 (7): 718–730.

Frederickson, N. and Cline, T. (2015) *Special Educational Needs, Inclusion and Diversity* (3rd ed.). Maidenhead: Open University Press.

Fuchs, D. and Fuchs, L. S. (1994) *What's "Special" About Special Education?* Available at http://files.eric.ed.gov/fulltext/ED379817.pdf Accessed 21st December 2016.

Garrick Duhaney, L. M. (2012) Understanding and addressing barriers to the implementation of inclusive education in C. Boyle and K. Topping (eds) *What Works in Inclusion?* Maidenhead: Open University Press.

Gathercole, S. E. and Alloway, T. P. (2008) *Working Memory in the Classroom: A Practical Guide for Teachers*. London: Sage.

Gelman, R. and Gallistel, C. R. (1978) *The Child's Understanding of Number*. Cambridge, MA: Harvard University Press.

Gillard, D. (2009) Us and them: A history of pupil grouping policies in England's schools. *Forum* 51 (1): 49–72.

Gillman, M., Heyman, B. and Swain, J. (2000) What's in a name? The implications of diagnosis for people with learning difficulties and their family carers. *Disability and Society* 15 (3): 389–409.

Gillum, J. (2014) Assessment with children who experience difficulty in mathematics. *Support for Learning* 29 (3): 275–291.

Glover, G. and Ayub, M. (2010) *How People With Learning Difficulties Die: Improving Health and Lives: Learning Difficulties Observatory*. Available at www.improvinghealthandlives.org.uk/gsf.php5?f=8586.

Goering, S. (2010) Revisiting the relevance of the social model of disability. *The American Journal of Bioethics* 10 (1): 54–55.

Goodey, C. (2011) *A History of Intelligence and Intellectual Disability: The Shaping of Psychology in Early Modern Europe*. Farnham, UK: Ashgate.

Goodley, D., Runswick-Cole, K. and Liddiard, K. (2015) The dishuman child. *Discourse: Studies in the Cultural Politics of Education*. http://dx.doi.org/10.1080/01596306.2015.1075731.

Goward, P. and Gething, L. (2005) Independence, reciprocity and resilience in G Grant, P Goward, M Richardson and P Ramcharan (eds) *Learning disability: a life cycle approach to valuing people*. Maidenhead. Open University Press.

Grant, G., Goward, P., Richardson, M. and Ramcharan, P. (eds) (2005) *Learning Disability: A Life Cycle Approach to Valuing People*. Maidenhead: Open University Press.

Grove, N. (2012) Story, agency, and meaning making: Narrative models and the social inclusion of people with severe and profound intellectual disabilities. *Journal of Religion, Disability & Health* 16 (4): 334–351.

Grove, N. (2013) Speaking and listening in the national curriculum: Comments on the revised programme of study. *The SLD Experience* 66: 3–5.

Grove, N. (2014) Personal oral narratives in a special school curriculum: An analysis of key documents. *British Journal of Special Education* 41 (1): 6–24.

Grove, N. and Park, K. (1996) Odyssey now: A drama project for people with severe and profound learning disabilities based on Homer's Odyssey. *The SLD Experience* 15: 13–14.

Gunnþórsdóttir, H. (2014) The Teacher in an Inclusive School: Exploring Teachers' Construction of Their Meaning and Knowledge Relating to Their Concepts and Understanding of Inclusive Education. Dissertation submitted in Partial Fulfilment of a Ph.D.degree. University of Iceland School of Education.

Hall, T. E., Meyer, A. and Rose, D. H. (2012) An introduction to universal design for learning: Questions and answers in T. E. Hall, A. Meyer and D. H. Rose (eds) *Universal Design for Learning in the Classroom: Practical Applications*. New York: Guildford Press.

Hansen, J. H. (2012) Limits to inclusion. *International Journal of Inclusive Education* 16 (1): 89–98.

Hart, S. and Drummond, M. (2014) Learning without limits: Constructing a pedagogy free from determinist beliefs about ability in L. Florian (ed) *The Sage Handbook of Special Education* (2nd ed.). London: Sage.

Hart, S., Drummond, M. and McIntyre, D. (2007) Learning without limits in L. Florian (ed) *The Sage Handbook of Special Education* London: Sage, 499–514.

Hewett, D. (1998) Challenging behaviour is normal in P. Lacey and C. Ouvry (eds) *People With Profound and Multiple Learning Difficulties*. London: David Fulton.

Hewett, D. (March, 2006) The most important and complicated learning: That's what play is for! ICAN. *Talking Point*. Available at www.talkingpoint.org.uk. Accessed 6th February 2009.

Hill, V., Croydon, A., Greathead, S., Kenny, L., Yates, R. and Pellicano, E. (2016) Research methods for children with multiple needs: Developing techniques to facilitate all children and young people to have 'a voice'. *Educational & Child Psychology* 33 (3): 26–43.

HMG/DH. (2011) *No Health Without Mental Health: A Cross Government Mental Health Outcomes Strategy for People of All Ages*. London: Her Majesty's Government/Department of Health.

Hodkinson, A. (2012) Illusionary Inclusion: What went wrong with new labour's landmark educational policy? *British Journal of Special Education* 39 (1): 4–10.

Hodkinson, A. (2016) *Key Issues in Special Educational Needs and Inclusion*. London: Sage.

Hollingsworth, K. (2013) Theorising children's rights in youth justice: The significance of autonomy and foundational rights. *The Modern Law Review* 76 (6): 1046–1069.

Holt, G., Gratsa, A., Bouras, N., Joyce, T., Spiller, M.J. and Hardy, S. (2006) *Guide to Mental Health for Families and Carers of People with Intellectual Disabilities*. London. Jessica Kingsley.

Hornby, G. (2015) Inclusive special education: Development of a new theory for the education of children with special educational needs and disabilities. *British Journal of Special Education* 42 (3): 234–256.

Hulme, C., Goetz, K., Brigstocke, S., Nash, H. M., Lerva, A. and Snowling, M. J. (2013) The growth of reading skills in children with Down syndrome. *Developmental Science* 15 (3): 320–329.

Hurley, R. L. (1969) *Poverty and Mental Retardation, a Causal Relationship*. New York: Random House.

Imray, P. (2008) *Turning the Tables on Challenging Behaviour: A Practitioner's Perspective to Transforming Challenging Behaviours in Children, Young People and Adults With SLD, PMLD or ASD*. London: Routledge.

Imray, P. (2013a) Can the P scales give a sufficient and accurate assessment of progress for pupils and students with severe or profound learning difficulties. *The SLD Experience* 66: 17–25.

Imray, P. (2013b) Alternatives assessment and pupil progress indicators to the P scales for pupils and students with SLD or PMLD. *The SLD Experience* 67: 7–16.

Imray, P. (2015) Literacy, phonics, and the SLD learner. *The SLD Experience* 72: 8–11.

Imray, P., Colley, A., Holdsworth, T., Carver, G. and Savory, P. (in print) *Listening to Behaviours: An Exercise in Adopting a Capabilities Approach to Education*. The SLD Experience.

Imray, P. and Hewett, D. (2015) Challenging behaviour and the curriculum in P. Lacey, R. Ashdown, P. Jones, H. Lawson and M. Pipe (eds) *The Routledge Companion to Severe, Profound and Multiple Learning Difficulties*. London: Routledge.

Imray, P. and Hinchcliffe, V. (2012) Not fit for purpose: A call for separate and distinct pedagogies as part of a national framework for those with severe and profound learning difficulties. *Support for Learning* 27 (4): 150–157.

Imray, P. and Hinchcliffe, V. (2014) *Curricula for Teaching Children and Young People With Severe or Profound Learning Difficulties*. London: Routledge.

Jackson, L. (2014) What legitimizes segregation? The context of special education discourse: A response to Ryndak et al. *Research and Practice for Persons With Severe Disabilities* 39 (2): 156–160.

Johnson, K. and Walmsley, J. (2010) *People With Intellectual Disabilities: Towards a Good Life?* Bristol: The Policy Press.

Jordan, R. (2001) *Autism With Severe Learning Difficulties*. London: Souvenir Press.

Jordan, R. (2005) Autistic spectrum disorders in A. Lewis and B. Norwich (eds) *Special Teaching for Special Teaching? Pedagogies for Inclusion*. Maidenhead: Open University Press.

Katz, J., Porath, M., Bendu, C. and Epp, B. (2012) Diverse voices: Middle years students' insights into life in inclusive classrooms. *Exceptionality Education International* 22 (1): 2–16.

Kauffman, J. M. (2002) *Education Deform: Bright People Sometimes Say Stupid Things About Education*. Laham, MD: Scarecrow Press.

Kauffman, J. M. and Badar, J. (2014a) Instruction, not inclusion, should be the central issue in special education: An alternative view from the USA. *Journal of International Special Needs Education* 17 (1): 13–20.

Kauffman, J. M. and Badar, J. (2014b) Better thinking and clearer communication will help special education. *Exceptionality: A Special Education Journal* 22 (1): 17–32.

Kearey, A-M. (2016) *Holding Complexity in your Hands: being the parent of a severely disabled child*. Lecture to Undergraduate Students. University of East London.

Kelly, A. V. (2009) *The Curriculum: Theory and Practice*. London: Sage.

Klingberg, T. (2009) *The Overflowing Brain: Information Overload and the Limits of Working Memory*. Oxford: Oxford University Press.

Lacey, P. (2009) Developing thinking and problem solving skills. *The SLD Experience* 54: 19–24.

Lacey, P., Ashdown, R., Jones, P., Lawson, H. and Pipe, M. (eds) (2015) *The Routledge Companion to Severe, Profound and Multiple Learning Difficulties*. London: Routledge.

Lacey, P. and Ouvrey, C. (eds) (1998) *People With Profound & Multiple Learning Disabilities*. London: David Fulton.

Lacey, P. and Scull, J. (2015) Inclusive Education for Learners with Severe, Profound and Multiple Learning Difficulties in England in E A. West (ed.) *Including Learners with Low-Incidence Disabilities (International Perspectives on Inclusive Education, Volume 5)*. Bingley, Yorkshire. Emerald Group Publishing Limited.

Lauchlan, F. and Boyle, C. (2007) Is the use of labels in special education helpful? *Support for Learning* 22 (1): 36–42.

Lauchlan, F. and Fadda, R. (2012) The Italian model of full inclusion: Origins and current directions in C. Boyle and K. Topping (eds) *What Works in Inclusion?* Maidenhead: Open University Press.

Lauchlan, F. and Greig, S. (2015) Educational inclusion in England: Origins, perspectives and current directions. *Support for Learning* 30 (1): 69–82.

Lawson, H. and Byers, R. (2015) Curriculum models, issues and tensions in P. Lacey, R. Ashdown, P. Jones, H. Lawson and M. Pipe (eds) *The Routledge Companion to Severe, Profound and Multiple Learning Difficulties*. London: Routledge.

Lewis, A. (1991) Changing views of special educational needs. *Education 3-13* 27 (3): 45–50.

Lewis, A. and Norwich, B. (eds) (2005) *Special Teaching for Special Children?* Maidenhead. Open University Press.

Locke, J., Ishijima, E H., Kasari, C. and London, N. (2010) Loneliness, friendship quality and the social networks of adolescents with high-functioning autism in an inclusive school setting. *Journal of Research in Special Educational Needs* 10 (2): 74–81.

Longhorn, F. (1988) *A Sensory Curriculum for Very Special People*. London: Souvenir.

Loreman, T. (2013) Canadian pre-service teachers and exclusion: Views and origins. In P. Jones (ed.). *Infusing insider perspectives into inclusive teacher learning: Potentials and challenges*. Abingdon, UK: Routledge.

Loreman, T., Deppeler, J. and Harvey, D. (2010) *Inclusive Education: Supporting Diversity in the Classroom*. Abingdon: Routledge.

McConkey, R. and McEvoy, J. (1986) Games for learning to count. *British Journal of Special Education* 13 (2): 59–62.

McGuire, J. M., Scott, S. S. and Shaw, S. F. (2006) Universal design and its applications in educational environments. *Remedial and Special Education* 27 (3): 166–175.

Male, D. (2015) Learners with SLD and PMLD: Provision, policy and practice in P. Lacey, R. Ashdown, P. Jones, H. Lawson and M. Pipe (eds) *The Routledge Companion to Severe Profound and Multiple Learning Difficulties*. London: Routledge.

Martin, T. and Alborz, A. (2014) Supporting the education of pupils with profound intellectual and multiple disabilities: The views of teaching assistants regarding their own learning and development needs. *British Journal of Special Education* 41 (3): 309–327.

Mastropieri, M. A. and Scruggs, T. E. (2010) *The Inclusive Classroom: Strategies for Effective Differentiated Instruction* (4th ed.). Upper Saddle River, NJ: Pearson Education.

Mencap. (2016) *New Research Highlights How Public Attitudes Contribute to Just 5.8% of People With a Learning Disability in Paid Work*. Available at www.men|cap.org.uk/press-release/new-research-highlights-how-public-attitudes-contribute-just-58-people-learning Accessed 23rd December 2016.

Michaud, K. and Scruggs, T. E. (2012) Inclusion in the United States: Theory and practice in C. Boyle and K. Topping (eds) *What Works in Inclusion?* Maidenhead: Open University Press.

Mock, D. and Kauffman, J. (2005) The delusion of full inclusion in J. Jacobson, R. Foxx and J. Mulick (eds) *Controversial Therapies for Developmental Disabilities: Fad, Fashion and Science in Professional Practice*. Mahwah, NJ: Lawrence Erlbaum Associates.

Murayama, H., Fujiwara, Y. and Kawachi, I. (2012) Social capital and health: A review of prospective multilevel studies. *Journal of Epidemiology* 22: 179–187.

Ndaji, F. and Tymms, P. (2009) *The P Scales: Assessing the Progress of Children With Special Educational Needs*. London: Wiley-Blackwell.

Nes, K. (2004) Quality versus equality? Inclusion politics in Norway at century's end. *Counterpoints* 270: 125–140.

Niemeyer, M. (2014) The right to inclusive education in Germany. *The Irish Community Development Law Journal* 3 (1): 49–64.

Nind, M. (2005) Introduction: Models and practice in inclusive curricula in M. Nind, J. Rix, K. Sheehy and K. Simmons (eds) *Curriculum and Pedagogy in Inclusive Education*. Abingdon: RoutledgeFarmer.

Nind, M. and Hewett, D. (1988) Interaction as curriculum. *British Journal of Special Education* 15 (2): 55–57.

Nind, M., Flewitt, R. and Payler, J. (2010) The social experience of early childhood for children with learning disabilities: Inclusion competence and agency. *British Journal of Sociology of Education* 31, 653–670.

Norwich, B. (2008) *Dilemmas of Difference, Inclusion and Disability: International Perspectives and Future Directions*. Abingdon, Oxford: Routledge.

Norwich, B. (2012) How inclusion policy works in the UK (England): Successes and issues in C. Boyle and K. Topping (eds) *What Works in Inclusion?* Maidenhead: Open University Press.

Norwich, B. (2013) *Addressing Tensions and Dilemmas in Inclusive Education*. London: Routledge.

Norwich, B. and Lewis, A. (2005) How specialized is teaching pupils with disabilities and difficulties? in A. Lewis and B. Norwich (eds) *Special Teaching for Special Children?* Maidenhead: Open University Press.

Nussbaum, M. C. (2004) *Hiding From Humanity: Disgust, Shame and the Law*. Princeton, NJ: Princeton University Press.

Nussbaum, M. C. (2007) *Frontiers of Justice – Disability, Nationality, Species Membership*. Cambridge, MA: Harvard University Press.

Nussbaum, M. C. (2009) The Capabilities of People with Cognitive Disabilities. *Metaphilosophy* 40: 331–351.

Nussbaum, M. C. (2010) The capabilities of people with cognitive disabilities in E. F. Kittay and L. Carlson (eds) *Cognitive Disability and Its Challenge to Moral Philosophy*. Oxford: Wiley-Blackwell.

Nussbaum, M. C. (2011a) *Creating Capabilities: The Human Development Approach*. Cambridge, MA: Belknap Press.

Nussbaum, M. C. (2011b) Perfectionist liberalism and political liberalism. *Philosophy and Public Affairs* 39 (1): 3–45.

Nye, J., Fluck, M. and Buckley, S. J. (2001) Counting and cardinal understanding in children with Down syndrome and typically developing children. *Down Syndrome Research and Practice* 7 (2): 68–78.

O'Brien, J. (2016) *Don't Send Him in Tomorrow: Shining a Light on the Marginalised, Disenfranchised and Forgotten Children of Today's Schools*. Carmarthen: Independent Thinking Press.

OECD. (2006) PISA 2003 sample questions quoted in Clausen-May T (2007) *International mathematics tests and pupils with special educational needs. British Journal of Special Education* 34 (3): 154–161.

Ofsted. (2015) *Maintained Schools and Academies: Inspections and Outcomes September 2014 to August 2015*. Available at www.gov.uk/government/statistics/maintained-schools-and-academies-inspections-and-outcomes-sep-2014-to-aug-2015 Accessed 17th February 2016.

Oliver, M. (1990) *The Politics of Disablement*. Basingstoke: Palgrave Macmillan.

Oliver, M. (1996) *Understanding Disability: From Theory to Practice*. Basingstoke: Palgrave Macmillan.

ONS. (2016) *Unemployment: Office for National Statistics* Available at www.ons.gov.uk/employmentandlabourmarket/peoplenotinwork/unemployment Accessed 6th December 2016.

Orr, R. (2016) Available at sld-forum@lists.education.gov.uk Accessed 5th November 2016.

Ouvry, C. (1987) *Educating Children With Profound Handicaps*. Kidderminster: BIMH Publications.

Pagliano, P. (2001) *Using a Multisensory Environment: A Practical Guide for Teachers*. London: David Fulton.

Park, K. (2010) *Interactive Storytelling: Developing Inclusive Stories for Children and Adults*. Bicester: Speechmark.

Paterson, S. J., Girelli, L., Butterworth, B. and Karmiloff-Smith, A. (2006) Are numerical impairments syndrome specific? Evidence from Williams syndrome and Down's syndrome. *Journal of Child Psychology and Psychiatry* 47 (2): 190–204.

Pease, L. (2008) Curriculum success for learners with complex needs. *Insight* 13: 10–13.

Perry, D., Hammond, L., Marston, G., Gaskell, S. and Eva, J. (2011) *Caring for the Physical and Mental Health of People With Learning Disabilities*. London: Jessica Kingsley.

Piaget, J. (1952) *The Origins of Intelligence in Children*. New York: International Press.

Pick, D. (1989) *Faces of Degeneration: A European Disorder*. Cambridge: Cambridge University Press.

Pinney, A. (2017) *Understanding the needs of disabled children with complex needs or life-limiting conditions*. London. Council for Disabled Children/True Colours Trust.

Polat, F. (2011) Inclusion in education: A step towards social justice. *International Journal of Educational Development* 31 (1): 50–58.

Porter, J. (2000) The Important of creating a mathematical environment. *The SLD Experience* 26: 16–17.

Porter, J. (2005a) Awareness of number in children with severe and profound learning difficulties: Three exploratory case studies. *British Journal of Learning Difficulties* 33 (3): 97–101.

Porter, J. (2005b) Severe learning difficulties in A. Lewis and B. Norwich (eds) *Special Teaching for Special Teaching? Pedagogies for inclusion*. Maidenhead: Open University Press.

Porter, J. (2010) Developing number awareness and children with severe and profound learning difficulties. *The SLD Experience* 57: 3–7.

Pring, T. (2004) Ask a silly question: Two decades of troublesome trials. *International Journal of Language and Communication Disorders* 39 (3): 285–302.

QCA. (2001) *Planning, Teaching and Assessing the Curriculum for Pupils With Learning Difficulties*. London: Qualifications and Curriculum Authority.

QCA. (2004) *Planning, Teaching and Assessing the Curriculum for Pupils With Learning Difficulties*. London: Qualifications and Curriculum Authority.

QCA. (2009) *The P Scales: Level Descriptors P1 to P8*. London: Qualification and Curriculum Authority.

QCDA. (2009) *Planning, Teaching and Assessing the Curriculum for Pupils With Learning Difficulties: General Guidance*. London: Qualifications and Curriculum Development Agency.

Rayner, M. (2011) The curriculum for children with severe and profound learning difficulties at Stephen Hawking School. *Support for Learning* 26 (1): 25–32.

Reindal, S. M. (2010) What is the purpose? Reflections on inclusion and education from a capabilities perspective. *European Journal of Special Needs Education* 25 (1): 1–12.

Reiser, R. (2014) *Disability Equality: Medical Model/Social Model*. Available at www.worldofinclusion.com/medical_social_model.htm.

Reversi, S., Langher, V., Crisafulli, V. and Ferri, R. (2007) The quality of disabled students' school integration: A research experience in the Italian state school system. *School Psychology International* 28 (4): 403–418.

Rhodes, G. (2016) Have you heard the one about the comedian and his autistic son? *The Guardian Newspaper: Family*. Saturday 10th September 2016, 1–2.

Riddick, B. (2009) P scales – The context in F. Ndaji and P. Tymms (ed) *The P Scales: Assessing the Progress of Children With Special Educational Needs*. London: Wiley-Blackwell.

Rix, J., Hall, K., Nind, M., Sheehy, K. and Wearmouth, J. (2009) What pedagogical approaches can effectively include children with special educational needs in mainstream classrooms? A systematic literature review. *Support for Learning* 24 (2): 86–96.

Robbins, B. (2000) Does teaching numeracy lead to mathematical learning? *The SLD Experience* 26: 9–12.

Robertson, C. (2015) Changing special educational needs and disability legislation and policy: Implications for learners with SLD/PMLD in P. Lacey, R. Ashdown, P. Jones, H. Lawson and M. Pipe (eds) *The Routledge Companion to Severe Profound and Multiple Learning Difficulties*. London: Routledge.

Robinson, D. (2014) Developing Initial Teacher Education for Special Educational Needs, Disability and Inclusive Practices. Unpublished Thesis. Milton Keynes. Open University.

Robinson, K. and Aronica, L. (2015) *Creative Schools: Revolutionizing Education From the Ground Up*. London: Penguin.

Roch, M. and Jarrold, C. (2008) A comparison between word and nonword reading in Down syndrome: The role of phonological awareness. *Journal of Communication Disorders* 41: 305–318.

Rochford Review. (2016) The Rochford Review: Final Report. Review of Assessment for Pupils Working Below the Standard of National Curriculum Tests. *Standards and Testing Agency*. Available at www.gov.uk/government/publications/rochford-review-final-report.

Rogers, C. (2016) *Intellectual Disability and Being Human*. Oxford: Routledge.

Rose, D. H., Gravel, J. W. and Gordon, D. T. (2014) Universal Design for Learning in L. Florian (ed.) *The Sage Handbook of Special Education* (2nd ed.). London: Sage.

Rose, D. H., Meyer, A. and Hitchcock, C. (eds) (2005). *The Universally Designed Classroom: Accessible Curriculum and Digital Technologies*. Cambridge, MA: Harvard University Press.

Rose, R. and Howley, M. (2007) *The Practical Guide to Special Educational Needs in Inclusive Primary Classrooms*. London: Sage.

Runswick-Cole, K. (2011) Time to end the bias towards inclusion. *British Journal of Special Education* 38 (3): 112–119.

Ryndak, D., Jackson, L. B. and White, J. M. (2013) Involvement and progress in the general curriculum for students with extensive support needs: K – 12 inclusive-education research and implications for the future. *Inclusion* 1 (1): 28–49.

Salt, T. (2010) *Salt Review: Independent Review of Teacher Supply for Pupils With Severe, Profound and Multiple Learning Difficulties (SLD and PMLD)*. Nottingham: DCSF.

Sebba, J., Byers, R. and Rose, R. (1993) *Redefining the Whole Curriculum for Pupils With Learning Difficulties*. London: David Fulton.

Seligman, M. (1975) *Helplessness: On Depression, Development and Death*. San Francisco, CA: W. H. Freeman.

Sen, A. (1985) *Commodities and Capabilities*. Amsterdam: North-Holland.

Sen, A. (1992) *Inequality Reexamined*. Oxford: Clarendon Press.

Sen, A. (1999) *Commodities and Capabilities*. New Delhi, India: Oxford University Press.

Sen, A. (2005) Human rights and capabilities. *Journal of Human Development* 6 (2): 151–166.

Shakespeare, T. (2006) *Disability Rights and Wrongs*. London: Routledge.

Sharma, A. and Cockerill, H. (2014) *Mary Sheridan's From Birth to Five Years* (4th ed.). London: Routledge.

Sharma, U. and Sokal, L. (2015) The impact of a teacher education course on pre-service teachers' beliefs about inclusion: An international comparison. *Journal of Research in Special Educational Needs* 15 (4): 276–284.

Shattuck, P. T., Orsmond, G. I., Wagner, M. and Cooper, B. P. (2011) Participation in social activities among adolescents with an autism spectrum disorder. *PLoS One*, 6 (11): e27176. doi:10.1371/journal.pone.0027176.

Shogren, K. A., Gross, J. M., Forber-Pratt, A. J., Francis, G. L., Satter, A. L., Blue-Banning, M. and Hill, C. (2015) The perspectives of students with and without disabilities on inclusive schools. *Research and Practice for Persons With Severe Disabilities* 40: 173–181.

Shuttleworth, M. A. (2013) Inclusion is. . .: Musing and conversations about the meaning of inclusion in A. Azzopardi (ed) *Youth: Responding to Lives*. Dordrecht, The Netherlands: Sense Publishers.

Simmons, B. and Bayliss, P. (2007) The role of special schools for children with profound and multiple learning difficulties: Is segregation always best? *British Journal of Special Education* 34 (1): 19–24.

Simmons, B. and Watson, D. (2014) *The PMLD Ambiguity: Articulating the Life-Worlds of Children With Profound and Multiple Learning Disabilities*. London: Karnac.

Sissons, M. (2010) *MAPP: Mapping and Assessing Personal Progress*. North Allerton: The Dales School.

Skidmore, D. (1996) Towards an integrated theoretical framework for research in special educational needs. *European Journal of Special Needs Education* 11 (1): 33–42.

Slee, R. (2010) *The Irregular School*. Abingdon: Routledge.

Slee, R. (2012) Inclusion in schools: What is the task? in C. Boyle and K. Topping (eds) *What Works in Inclusion?* Maidenhead: Open University Press.

Sokal, L. and Katz, J. (2015) Oh, Canada: Bridges and barriers to inclusion in Canadian schools. *Support for Learning* 30 (1): 42–54.

Solomon, A. (2012) *Far from the tree: Parents, children and the search for identity*. New York. Simon and Schuster.

Stansfeld, S. A. (2006) Social support and social cohesion in M. Marmot and R. G. Wilkinson (eds) *Social Determinants of Health*. Oxford: Oxford University Press.

Staves, L. (2001) *Mathematics for Children With Severe and Profound Learning Difficulties*. London: David Fulton.

Swain, J. and French, S. (2004) Towards and affirmation model of disability. *Disability and Society* 15 (4): 569–582.

Swanson, H. L. and Jerman, O. (2006) Maths disabilities: A selective meta-analysis of the literature. *Review of Educational Research* 6 (2): 249–274.

Taylor, B. (2014) *The Last Asylum – a Memoir of Madness in Our Times*. London: Penguin.

Terzi, L. (2010) *Justice and Equality in Education: A Capability Perspective on Disability and Special Educational Needs*. London: Continuum.

Thomas, G. and Loxley, A. (2007) *Deconstructing Special Education and Constructing Inclusion*. Berkshire: Open University Press.

Thomas, G. and O'Hanlon, C. (2005) Series editors preface in A. Lewis and B. Norwich (eds) *Special Teaching for Special Children*. Maidenhead: Open University Press.

Topping, K. (2012) Conceptions of inclusion: Widening ideas in C. Boyle and K. Topping (eds) *What Works in Inclusion*. Maidenhead: Open University Press.

Trussler, S. and Robinson, D. (2015) *Inclusive Practice in the Primary School*. London: Sage.

Uchino, B. N. (2006) Social support and health: A review of physiological processes potentially underlying links to disease outcomes. *Journal of Behavioral Medicine* 29: 377–387.

UNESCO. (1994) *The Salamanca Statement and Framework for Action on Special Needs*. Paris: UNESCO Education.

United Nations. (1989) *Convention on the Rights of the Child*. New York: United Nations.

Uzgiris, I. and Hunt, J. (1975) *Assessment in Infancy: Ordinal Scales of Psychological Development*. Urbana: University of Illinois Press.

Vanier, J. (1998) *Becoming Human*. Toronto: House of Anansi Press.

Victoria School. (2009) *The Victoria School MSI Curriculum*. Available at www.sense.org.uk/content/msi-curriculum.

WAG. (2006) *Routes for Learning: Assessment Materials for Learners With Profound Learning Difficulties and Additional Disabilities*. Cardiff: Welsh Assembly Government.

Walton, E. (2016) *The Language of Inclusive Education*. London: Routledge.

Ware, J. (1994) Implementing the 1988 Act with pupils with PMLDs in J. Ware (ed) *Educating Children With Profound and Multiple Learning Difficulties*. London: David Fulton.

Ware, J. (2003) *Creating a Responsive Environment for People With Profound and Multiple Learning Difficulties*. London: David Fulton.

Ware, J. (2005) Profound and multiple learning difficulties, in Lewis A and Norwich B (eds) *Special Teaching for Special Teaching? Pedagogies for inclusion*. Maidenhead. Open University Press.

Ware, J. (2014) Curriculum considerations in meeting the educational needs of learners with severe intellectual disabilities in L. Florian (ed) *The Sage Handbook of Special Education* (2nd ed.). London: Sage.

Warnock, M. (1975) *Report of the Committee of Enquiry Into the Education of Handicapped Children*. London: HMSO.

Warnock, M. (2005) Special educational needs: A new look in L. Terzi (ed) *Special Educational Needs*. London: Continuum.

Wearmouth, J. (2011) *Special Educational Needs – the Basics*. London: Routledge.

Webster, R. and Blatchford, P. (2014) Who has the responsibility for teaching pupils with SEN in mainstream primary schools? Implications for policy arising from the 'Making a Statement' study. *Journal of Research in Special Educational Needs* 14 (3): 196–200.

Wedell, K. (1995) Making inclusive education ordinary. *British Journal of Special Education* 22 (3): 100–104.

Wendelborg, C. and Kvello, O. (2010) Perceived social acceptance and peer intimacy among children with disabilities in regular schools in Norway. *Journal of Applied Research in Intellectual Disabilities* 23: 143–153.

Westwood, P. (2015) *Common-Sense Methods for Children With Special Educational Needs*. London: Routledge.

Whitehurst, T. (2007) Liberating silent voices: Perspectives of children with profound and complex learning needs on inclusion. *British Journal of Learning Disabilities* 35: 55–61.

Wolfensberger, W. (1983) Social role valorization: A proposed new term for the principle of normalization. *Mental Retardation* 21 (6): 234–239.

Wolff, J. and de Shallit, A. (2007) *Disadvantage*, Oxford: Oxford University Press.

Author index

Subject index

Printed in Great Britain
by Amazon